To Tom

EXITS AND ENTRANCES

Very Rev. J — R Leo +
Nov. 2010

James R. Leo

"All the world's a stage, and all the men and women merely players: they have their exits and their entrances; and one man in his time plays many parts." William Shakespeare, *"As You Like It" (Act II, Scene VII).*

To order additional copies of this book, contact:
Xlibris Corporation
1-888-795-4274
www.Xlibris.com
Orders@Xlibris.com
51207

CONTENTS

To my wife, our sons, and their families

WHAT READERS ARE SAYING

In this luminescent memoir Dean Leo, a raconteur for God, charmingly threads a serendipitous line between the reverent and irreverent. *Exits and Entrances* s catches a glimpse of one man's working faith. We see a young man surprising even himself by blurting out in public his intent to enter the priesthood. We see a wounded priest ministering to a dear friend at the time of death. We see a workaday priest caught up in the pomp and intrigue of the funeral of the Duchess of Windsor. We see a faithful servant reach out to casual acquaintances met mall walking. We share his memories of several faith communities including two great Cathedrals. And as we see him reminisce and explore his life and faith, we gain insight into our own life decisions and faith experiences. This is indeed a good read.

Mary Ann Weiss, Trinity Episcopal Church,
Covington, Kentucky

Achieving surprising depth and breadth in compact form, *Exits and Entrances* is the author's reflections on the time he has spent in the ministry and, in an oblique way, his youth. It is the intimate style in which he writes and the universal nature of his joys, obstacles, thoughts, and adventures that makes this book so meaningful. Each chapter recreates a compelling event or reflection that is singularly satisfying, yet compels the reader to seek more. If you want to know what goes on in the heart and mind of a good minister, this book will open your eyes.

Linda Berger, Christ Church Cathedral, Cincinnati, Ohio

I loved hearing about Paris and much more. From the world of commerce to Paris, London, Seville, and the high seas, chapter by chapter, *Exits and Entrances* provides a rare insight into the life and career of one very human clergyman. The Rev. James R. Leo is warm, wise, profound and funny, and so is his book. I recommend it to people of all faiths.

Natalie Denton, Grace Episcopal Church, Elmira, New York

CHAPTER ONE

THE DUCHESS OF WINDSOR

Alleluia! Thursday, April 24th is a day to live. Paris is showing off. Rain, dampness, mold, have lost the battle for our souls. This is a day of miracles and miracles come from heaven.

A street sweeper dressed in his green overalls, the city's uniform for its hired workers, has attached leafless tree branches to the end of a broomstick. With this homemade tool he and brothers in his trade push water down the gutter in a small flow made by turning on a faucet near the top of the street. Piles of debris, a torn beret, a dog leash, letters, soggy cigarettes, Kleenex, broken glass, an old sock, a used mitten, an empty worn purse and thousands of other cast off signs of French life, including lost hopes and faded dreams, all tossed onto Paris streets the night before, float down gutters to a grate at the bottom of the block and are swallowed into the bowels of the city—never to be seen or heard from again.

Today is different. A miracle is happening on our street. Our street sweeper is singing. He is singing "Lili Marlene". Yes, he is actually singing. It is a moment of grace. It is catching. It is beautiful. I am reborn.

A Frenchman wearing a blue striped English suit and vest, with a double vented suit coat, a silk tie, and a black bowler hat passes me where I am standing on the front steps of the Cathedral. A closed umbrella taps lightly with each step next to his shined black wingtips. I think of Maurice Chevalier. He passes me in my red cassock and says, *"Bonjour Monseigneur,"* and smiles. I quickly stand to attention. That aristocratic greeting requires more than a casual nod. I stand straight upright and in a clear strong voice, I reply *"Bon journée, Monsieur,"* and smile. Another miracle on this magic day.

Monsieur Nicolas across the street is setting tables for the approaching lunch hour at The Café George V. Madam is sitting at an empty rear table under the striped awning. She is clad in a huge white apron resembling a drapery and rapidly folding in creative shapes linen napkins for each table.

Monsieur holds a glass up to the light of the sky looking for smudges or other marks. Carefully wiping the glass he sets it on the table just above the knife next to the spoons. There is joy in the opening of an outdoor café on these spring days. Another Paris blessing.

Heavy window shutters sound like cars crashing as uniformed maids push them open. Neighbors wake up and in turn arise and open their shutters. The sun bursts into messy, damp apartments, which instantly become decorator's dreams on this elegant Avenue George V. Paris is waking up. At eight a.m. these steel monsters are the alarm clock for our street. In August when Parisians are in the South of France enjoying a vacation, only a few will sound their alarms, as many of the apartments are then empty. The George V is the home of the swells in the high rent district.

A few hours later lovers on the nearby banks of the Seine will be stretched on blankets at the end of the Avenue. They will sanctify and consecrate those banks as the morning ripens. Paris is experiencing a resurrection.

At lunchtime on these spring days, shapely French secretaries swan past outdoor cafes in seamless gossamer dresses. A sense of sexual excitement runs high, for young and old men alike. An accordion player standing on the sidewalk squeezes out French favorites in front of the tables. As he finishes, a pretty young girl, maybe six or seven years of age, moves among tables holding out a hat for any loose change for our noontime serenade. This musician will advance to the next café around the corner and repeat his performance. Within the next hour he will have stopped at three more places and have returned to our café to catch newcomers and play the same songs. Croissants, baguettes, cigarettes, wine and laughter fill our lives on this corner in Paris. Springtime gives new meanings to the word "Alleluia" as it anoints the Avenue George V. While we revel in joy, we are unaware of what is happening a ten-minute taxi ride away in a home in a discreet corner of the Bois de Boulogne.

Thursday, April 24th is a day for death. At 9:30 a.m. the phone rings, loudly, rudely bringing me back to reality. "Monsieur Le Doyen—come now, she is dying." It is Dr. Jean Thin, the long time physician for the Duchess of Windsor. I am being summoned from my towering fortress, the American Cathedral. Almighty God, the Cathedral, and the faith now step up to make their claim. A few hours ago I was filled with a sense of miracles and alleluias. Now I must heed the call to my vocation as a priest and the call of God to one of His people.

When I first arrived in Paris I heard about the phrase "*priorité a droite*". It means that drivers never have to look right when entering a circle or the many cross streets. Americans do not want to pay attention to this concept and do not know how to cope with the law and its strange reasoning. Driving in Paris is threatening even to Boston drivers. It will take maybe ten or fifteen minutes to reach the house in the Bois, depending on traffic and neurotic French drivers. So, how long will it take me today? *I don't know.*

Usually identification takes place at the front gate and George, the butler, walks down the drive to let me in. Today, the gate is open. I am expected. On entering the house alone, I walk up the spiral staircase to the next floor. The house is still. It is eerie. Is that death I sense?

No one comes here any longer. The doctor and I are the Duchess' only regular visitors. The Duke's drums are on a wall ledge halfway up the steps to the first floor, the drums that he would often play at parties. Now they are sad relics in the dust and quiet as I pass them on the steps. Useless sentries asleep under brooding stillness, they are waiting to beat retreat.

Climbing the remaining steps one passes through the Duke's bedchamber and a small den connecting the two bedrooms. Memorabilia and photographs of people and events of bygone days cover the walls. Wallis often sat in this room in the first days of her dementia to admire the garden. During those days she must have thought about her life and times with her royal husband, the once and future King of England.

The garden has memories of lavish summer evenings with the rich, the famous, lovers, friends loyal, and not so loyal, those royal and not so royal. Knights, Lords, and jackasses, would gather in this Garden of Eden. Eden is now weeds, crab grass, and ghosts.

The nurse is preparing the Duchess for my final visit. Covered by a thin sheet, Wallis lies amidst photos, memorabilia, and needlepoint pillows with images of her beloved pugs. Now a plain nightgown is her royal robe.

Among the photos is Wallis's godson, John Mortimer, the son of Linda and Henry Mortimer whom we knew when I was the rector at St. Mary's Church in Tuxedo Park, New York. The picture rests on a small round candle top table near a window not far from the bed, with some other photos of friends. All the photos are in silver frames of different sizes and shapes. My guess is that John is two or three years old at the time of this photo. The Mortimer family was an active member of the Tuxedo parish. Linda Mortimer is the daughter of Lord and Lady Metcalfe. Lord Metcalfe was the Best Man at the Duke's wedding. He was known among friends as "Fruity". Call someone Fruity today and you might end up with a black eye. The English give strange names to their friends and their desserts. Americans find it amusing. Linda's husband Henry is an American who wishes he could have been a titled Englishman. He nevertheless acts with style the part of an English squire. We spent many happy hours with the Mortimer family in the nineties. They would in a few days accompany us to Windsor Castle for the funeral.

Going immediately to Wallis' bedside, one sees the cause for the Doctor's concern. Her heart is weak and she is breathing in a broken rhythm. She is unable to comprehend her surroundings. Death is approaching. Over many years, I was able to communicate with Wallis. On each visit I explained who I was and why I was with her. On these occasions I would recite the Lord's Prayer and say a suitable psalm or prayer while holding her hand.

Wallis twitches. She is anxious. I hold her hand and recite prayers slowly as on previous visits. Over time one develops a pattern, a way to communicate on a level not so dependent on words. Wallis cannot speak. She occasionally squeezes my hand or changes facial expressions in response to simple questions. I am positive she hears some of what is said this morning. On this occasion she squeezes my hand when hearing the Lord's Prayer.

Now Wallis is perspiring. She is agitated. I read from the eighth chapter of Paul's Letter to the Romans. To one who is dying, these are some of the greatest words ever written. *"Now I see through a glass darkly but then I shall see face to face."* She calms down. I calm down. There are times in my life I have read this inspiring chapter when anxious or disturbed. It never fails to give strength and a new presence of Jesus Christ.

After the healing words of Paul there is silence. I speak slowly:

"Wallis you are going home. Do not be afraid. It will be the most beautiful trip you will ever take. You are dressed and ready. You have not forgotten anything. You have all you need. You are beautiful. God is coming to greet you, to gently lead you into a kingdom of peace, good will, and love."

I hold her hand. I know she is at peace. I anoint her body with holy oil. In the name of the Church I forgive her sins known and unknown. Her eyes are shut, her hand limp.

Edward the VI and Wallis were considered the high priest and priestess of the hedonists. Neither would be compared to any of the saints, great or lesser, of the Church. Edward's 325-day reign as King was not worth noting. Wallis' social climbing and spending habits did not endear her to the blessed in the echelons of the Church. The couple was not admired. Many fawned over them. Few worshipped them. Their social activities were important to their lifestyle. In later years, their illness confined them. They were no longer a focus of the world's social scene.

Peers of the English government frowned upon Edward's expensive tastes and the choice of Wallis as his wife. The Anglican Church would not recognize the union because of Wallis' previous marriages and divorce. The king was considered the protector of the faith, the head of the established religion in the English realm. Yet Edward did not even attend Church. Churchill was livid about the King's apparent friendship with Adolph Hitler. People in high places and important English institutions disapproved of his choice of Wallis. The Queen Mother refused to speak with Wallis. She made her disfavor known to the public. These problems forced the famous abdication speech on December 11, 1936 when Edward VI abdicated the throne in favor of "the woman I love." The royal family never was eager to associate with her. She was a lonely soul who had few to support her in hours of need.

Wallis was a baptized Christian, a confirmed Episcopalian. In her broken condition I always encouraged her to turn her life over to the great shepherd of souls. I hoped and wanted to believe this turning in the last few weeks did help her find the peace that passes all understanding. A few days later at a news conference I was able to say to the English press corps that the Duchess was neither frightened nor unhappy in her last moments.

I leave her bedside and take one last look at her face that is now peaceful. I kiss her forehead and leave her room. I sit at the desk in the Duke's room where he signed the abdication papers years ago. This is the last time for me to minister to Wallis Simpson, the Duchess of Windsor. Dr. Thin has not yet arrived. I return to the Cathedral. The phone is ringing as I enter my office. It is George, her butler for 35 years. Dr. Thin has arrived and he is with the body of the Duchess whose death has now been confirmed. I am asked to return.

In the months to come, society columnists, lawyers, members of the royal family, and authors would discuss, argue and write about Wallis Simpson's significance to English and American history. A brash divorced American had married an English King, who in turn gave up his throne for this woman. Storybook romances usually fill hearts with joy and romance. In this case the perception was that the intruder from Baltimore, Maryland had stolen the King of England.

I return to the house, climbing the steps to her bedroom. Alone with her I say the prayers for the dead. At the end of these prayers I request the staff join me. These faithful followers worked in the house and were with the Duchess for years—her nurse, her hairdresser, her butler George and his wife, and of course, Dr. Thin. I liked George—a simple man in a pleasant sense of the word. He was always willing to help. The members of the press looking for a story never fooled him. Dr. Jean Thin, a doctor to the Duke and Duchess is not only a fine doctor, but also a man of common sense and Christian values. Wallis' nurses were several at any one time and varied over time. I did not know them as well as I knew Dr. Thin and George. These loyal people knew about the Duchess' problems and on occasion her difficult temper and manner. Fair-weather friends and sycophants deserted Wallis when she no longer provided them with social pleasures. Her staff did not. To the end they are loyal to the Duchess and to each other.

One who is not present at the end is a lady, now deceased, who defended and protected Wallis for years—Maitre Blum, the lawyer for the Duchess. This lawyer's ways are difficult, her manner brusque. I never met her personally but talked to her by phone. Maitre Blum was angry with the royal family for removing papers and books from the household after the Duke's death. The courts decreed that papers and books should be returned as rightfully belonging to Wallis Simpson. The items were returned. She fiercely protected her client. Maitre Blum permitted few individuals beyond the doctor, nurses, and me to see Wallis. If ever I get into legal trouble in France I would like to have a lawyer like Maitre Blum to represent me.

On that memorable morning I make the short drive back to the Cathedral to begin the preparation for a memorial service at the Cathedral. The Duke and Duchess claimed the Cathedral as their home church even though they seldom attended. The Anglican Church never gave ecclesiastical permission for the marriage. The royal couple was not welcomed in the two English parishes in Paris.

I have work ahead of me. People are looking over my shoulder. How shall I conduct the service? Some want the preparations their way. Fortunately, the Episcopal Church has the Book of Common Prayer, a diamond in our crown. Liturgical rites are inspired by centuries of traditional usage. I do not have to make up a service. Clergy are able to rely upon tradition and, at the same time, discourage family members, well meaning friends, or publicity seekers from directing the service. Often well-intentioned people want to use maudlin prayers and thoughts about death in the services that have little relationship to the Christian faith.

Security in Paris is always in my mind because of dangers to famous and controversial leaders of countries. These people who sometimes appeared at services required protection from disruptions. The upcoming memorial service could be a time of such a disruption. I want to keep a sense of calm. Questions are going to be asked in the next four days. I am one of the few people at this moment who know about the death. I have maybe an hour's grace before the phone will ring—only a short time to prepare myself before the world is notified. Then the press will be on the doorstep.

The first job is to call Queen Elizabeth and tell her of the death. In previous conversations I had assured Her Majesty's ambassador in France that I would notify her first when the Duchess dies. I have a special number and had called earlier in the morning to inform the secretary that the Duchess is expected to die during the day. I call her again an hour later with the news that the expected death has taken place. I never talk directly with the Queen but a secretary passes my news to her. The Queen is in the room at the time and thanks me for keeping her informed. She requests that I accompany the body to Windsor castle on her private plane with a detachment of guards. I am honored by this request and by her appreciation of my services.

I explain that I will accompany the body to a Paris airport but that I am needed for a memorial service for the Duchess in Paris the same day of the proposed flight to Windsor. The body is to lie in state for a time so I can arrive at a later date. She understands this and agrees that I should arrive in England for the burial in Frogmore, the royal cemetery at Windsor Great Park. As the Queen is requesting that I come to England and take part in the service at Windsor Castle the following Monday and lead the burial at Frogmore, I hear her in the background say to her secretary, "Please make sure Mrs. Leo attends the service. Transportation will be provided for her."

Later in the afternoon I begin writing a sermon for the Paris memorial service. Eulogies are difficult. It is wrong to have one person lying in the nave and another lying in the pulpit. In my homily, I spend time talking about Jesus. Funerals are not for the dead but for the living. Wallis is now in God's hands and there is nothing we can do at this point. I remind my own family that when I die the service will be for their benefit, not mine. I don't care what hymns are sung or what lessons are read. I won't be attending. I will be with someone else. Funeral services glorify God, not the deceased. When one pays attention to the funeral service he discovers that the service is about life. The burial office refers to life in the Kingdom. It is in the service of Baptism where one talks about death. A Christian dies at baptism and is raised to a new life in Christ.

In the afternoon Patsy joins me at the Duchess' home. She has never been in the house before and I want her to have a chance to see it. We enter the home together and wait downstairs until everything is ready on the second floor. I take these few minutes to show her the large rooms on the first floor. At midpoint on the stairway we pass the well-known drums. I am now called to the second floor to lead the pallbearers, a contingent of the Queens guards, to escort the body to a waiting hearse and return to England.

I stand in the driveway where an area has been roped off for press and television. A commentator and television crew from CBS asks me for an interview about the present events. This interview

16

appears on the nightly news program in the States. I have yet to speak to my parents or friends in the States about the recent events. My parents in Pennsylvania are stunned to see me on television. I had wanted to reach them, and tell them of events first in a phone call instead of having them receive information through a televised news program. Time is not on my side. Someone once told me that God made time and he made so much of it so that everyone will have enough to go around. Today, I question this belief!

The body of the Duchess will lie in state for a time in the chapel at Windsor. I will not return to England immediately but I accompany her body to Orly Airport in the hearse. Four French motorcycle policemen lead us. Traveling very fast with sirens and lights blazing and people staring from the sidewalks, we arrive at the airport where Ambassadors and dignitaries form a double line. I lead the body to the Queen's plane. This part of the funeral preparation is now over for Wallis and for me.

CHAPTER TWO

WINDSOR CASTLE

Patsy and I returned to Orly airport two days after the Duchess of Windsor's memorial service in Paris, in order to fly to London to be part of a service in the country where Wallis was loved and hated.

Reservations had been made at the reasonably priced Durrants Hotel in the center of London where the staff is so courteous and friendly that we fondly referred to it as our home in London. We arrived to discover a message from the BBC, which had tried to locate me in Paris, and had discovered the time of my arrival from the Cathedral receptionist. The BBC was requesting a press conference in the afternoon, with television coverage. I had never been a part of what I assumed would be a large press conference. I was nervous about the idea. Impulsively I agreed, and arranged a time later in the afternoon for the conference to take place in the Durrants Hotel.

I unpacked my bags and took a short walk in the neighborhood. Patsy had made an appointment at the hairdresser. I left her with the idea of meeting in the room in the afternoon for a cup of tea following the conference, which was to be held in about three hours. In the back of my head I heard warning bells. Was I getting into something I didn't know about? That was certain. Even though I was a public personality in the Cathedral, I was a stranger to this kind of publicity.

I left the hotel to walk around the neighborhood enjoying the sights and beginning to wonder what would be asked at the news conference. I started to fantasize. Grand ideas began to form in my mind. I pictured myself speaking to thousands of people all over the world from their television sets. What great words of wisdom would I impart?

Then it happened! The falling glob didn't hit me in the head with much force, but I felt its impact. When pigeon droppings fall from the sky, I am sure most fall unnoticed and nobody cares. Not so in this case. It was as though I had been targeted specifically. My head had not only been bombarded but also drenched. Fragments were now beginning to ooze down the front of my face. I searched vainly in my pockets for a Kleenex but found nothing. I seldom carry handkerchiefs or Kleenex, a habit I was to regret once more before this day had ended.

A wet and dirty front page of the London Times was lying in the gutter. There was nothing else I could do. I picked the paper up out of the gutter and wiped my head. This was a messy job. I took an immediate and intense dislike to the woman sitting on the park bench who had witnessed this event and was laughing. My fall from grace was complete, having followed the same downward trajectory as the pigeon's well-aimed shot. I returned to the hotel for a shower and a long shampoo, resolved to focus less on my imagined grandeur and more upon the task ahead.

The BBC news people were ready in the lobby. Desk clerks, bus boys and a few guests who wanted to see the events of the next half hour were also waiting and watching. The first questions were routine. I identified myself and stated how long I had known the Duchess and in what capacity. I was asked to explain her relationship to the Duke of Windsor. I explained that I never knew the Duke and had been there only to minister to a member of the congregation who was ill. I elaborated on this second point. For almost ten years I had visited the Duchess about once a month. On most of these occasions she received communion and prayed with me. She had been unable to speak. It was only through facial gestures, nods of the head, and by holding hands did we communicate. If she seemed anxious and troubled I did not use communion but said prayers and talked about how God was with her at all times. On several occasions we had communion together.

I was asked to elaborate on the famous emeralds that could not be located. I knew nothing about this topic and said this was the first I had heard of this subject. Once again I was asked about the personal life of the Duchess and if I knew anything about her love life in the past ten years. I clearly stated that I knew nothing about that subject and added that if I did, you would never hear it from me. At this, the members of the press picked up their cameras and left. My fifteen minutes of fame were over in five minutes. The reporters from the BBC were unhappy. I was unhappy. I felt misused. When I returned to the room Patsy warned, "Hurry up and get to the conference because you are about to be late."

"It's over," I said. My short career as a television personality had ended.

I now looked forward to having dinner with the Mortimers, knowing that we would be going to a nice place. They spend lifetimes in nice places. The four of us were driven the next morning from London to Windsor Castle in a large Bentley. We sat in the back seat where we had for our use, if we wished, a stocked bar and a television set. Today these items are commonplace in large limousines. It was not so common in London years ago. People stared at our magnificent automobile as we rolled through the London streets. Even today, I still look twice when I see a chauffeured Rolls Royce or Bentley passing and remember my brief journey in London.

Large crowds had gathered at the main entrance to Windsor Castle. Some had been invited to the funeral, while others were waiting to catch a glimpse of a Royal or a movie star or a known personality. We were stopped at the entrance where we were to show a pass to the guards at the gate. At that moment, The Very Reverend Michael Mann, the Dean of Windsor, walked in front of the car and raised his hand. Dean Mann was a friend of ours whom we had met on previous occasions. I opened the window and greeted him. He got into the car and was driven to the Deanery to have coffee and breakfast cakes.

Dean Mann then escorted the Mortimers to their pew in the nave of the Chapel. Jill Mann took Patsy to the stalls in the Choir area. Members of the Garter have private stalls in the Chapel. Patsy sat in Prince Charles' stall situated below the Queen. I proceeded with the clergy and choir procession and took a seat in the altar area.

I had been conducted to the sacristy area to don my liturgical vestments. For the first part of the service, which was the Burial Office, I lead the congregation in the reciting of the Psalm. Dean Mann said prayers, and the Archbishop of Canterbury gave the final blessing.

The absence at the service of the Queen Mother was noticeable. Others in the Royal Family were present. It seemed strange to me that not once was the Duchess' name used in the service. We seemed to be going through motions. There was no sense of grief. There was no sense of victory. There was no sense of healing. There was no sense of memories to talk about. The closure on Wallis Simpson's life had taken place years ago. The service on this day was an historic moment. That's all it was meant to be. We sang a concluding hymn and proceeded to the narthex with the Queen and other members of the family. I felt sad.

We progressed out of the chapel and gathered at the front steps to travel by car the short distance to Frogmore, the burial ground of the Royal Family in years past. If we had walked, we would have arrived sooner. I'm sure security is always a consideration for trips long and short. Passing Victoria and Albert's mausoleum the cars stopped at the plot where Wallis was to rest for time eternal. There were not many present—the Queen, Prince Philip, Prince Charles, Lady Diana, and some members of the Queen's guard. From Paris there was Dr Thin, Wallis' butler George, the hairdresser, and some others whom I did not know. Only these few were present. I began the Service of Interment. I made a point of mentioning Wallis' name in one of the ancient collects said at the graveside. Finally, the memorable words were spoken—"ashes to ashes and dust to dust, in sure and certain hope of the resurrection". The blessing and the interment were over.

The Queen began to wipe a few tears from her eyes. Immediately a member of her staff asked everyone to move away. In a later conversation with Dean Mann I asked why we had been requested to move away. He told me that no one is supposed to see the Queen shed a tear. I started to move to a distant point with the others. The Queen stopped me and asked me to remain. There were a few tears on her face. I reached in my pocket to find a handkerchief, but had nothing but a Kleenex. I had used it before. Once again I found myself at a loss because I did not carry a handkerchief. I could not offer The Queen of England a used tissue. The great lady reached into her pocketbook and used her own lace hanky to wipe away the few tears that had gathered. She said to me, pointing to the grave next to Wallis', "He is one I loved." We walked a few steps and stood next to Edward's plot. I recited a brief prayer for Edward VII, by rights the King of England, but never crowned because of the woman who now rested next to him. The Queen then said, "Dean

Leo, you have done a magnificent job over these many years and I thank you." I was both touched and elated. I could feel my own eyes getting watery. Where was that Kleenex?

The Queen wanted to meet the hairdresser and George and Dr. Thin who were standing at a distance and added that she would need me as a translator. If she knew how poor my French was she would not have asked that question. I said nothing but felt my stomach begin to churn. First, I introduced George and Dr. Thin. She then expressed her thanks in perfect French. I introduced Wallis's hairdresser. This humble, uneducated, and beautiful peasant approached the queen and knelt at her feet. The Queen offered her hand and asked her to stand and accept thanks for a job well done. This simple person from somewhere in the middle of Paris was having her finest moment, just as I had only a few minutes before. The four of us had received accolades from this great lady. What an honor to be thanked by the Queen of England! When the Queen departed, the four of us were elated beyond description. It was a time we would always remember.

After returning to the Deanery, I told Patsy of my experience and feelings and said I had to make a phone call. I searched for a quiet place and made a call to my parents in Bryn Mawr, Pennsylvania. I kidded my mother and informed her that for most of my life she had told me that I only made mistakes. The Queen of England had just told me that I had done a good job!

We spent the night at the Deanery in a glorious bedroom with high ceilings and large drapes from ceiling to floor. A small three-step ladder was used to climb into this huge bed and pull curtains that seemed to lock us in. Early in the morning with the sun coming up, I climbed down the ladder and went to the windows to pull ropes to open the vast drapes. Far away we could see a soldier with a large beaver hat standing on a high wall. I came back to the bed and climbed up the ladder and suggested to Patsy that we had a unique opportunity here. Being in this magnificent bed, in Windsor Castle no less, perhaps we should . . . . No, the man in the beaver hat might see us, Patsy pointed out nervously. So we compromised. I gave up any amorous ideas and together we arose and went to Church.

At seven a.m. we were a congregation of three—the Bishop, Patsy and me—at the daily communion service. Following the service, the Bishop volunteered to take us on a tour of the private rooms not yet open to the public, and it was an enormous treat to see half finished chapels, stone crypts, and niches in walls containing perhaps someone's remains. Who knows?

Finally, we were off to the airport for our return to Paris. The memories of those few days will always be with us. A bit of history had transpired and we were thankful to have been part of it.

CHAPTER THREE

A PRESIDENTIAL VISIT

Bastille Day, July 14th 1989, would be the 200th Anniversary of the French Revolution. Parades, concerts, soccer, the Tour de France, and other gala events would be staged during the month. Parisians adore their holidays. When Paris celebrates, the world watches and wishes it were here.

NATO leaders planned for a meeting of the heads of state during the week of Bastille Day. George Bush, our 41st President, would be coming to Paris. I had written to the President some time in March and asked him to participate in our Sunday service at the American Cathedral on that weekend. Early in June, my phone rang and I was informed that an advance team had arrived in Paris to visit the sites where the President would be present. They would like to visit with me the next day.

Two busloads of people arrived the next morning to talk with me and to walk around the Cathedral, a first indication that President Bush might actually be coming to our service. The press corps made up half of this advance; others were Secret Service. There was little admiration or respect between the two groups. These attitudes did not change on succeeding visits even though the individuals involved changed. It was apparent that the White House and the press did not trust each other. *Plus ca change, plus c'est la meme chose.*

After the visit I was assigned an embassy official who was to be the liaison between my office and the White House. I was beginning to think I was important. Patsy kept reminding me who I really was! The first benefit of the impending visit was that the next day the French Road Works resurfaced the access road in front of the Cathedral in anticipation of the visit.

The Secret Service team assigned to us made its first visit and met the staff. We were impressed with the group and became friends. Some stayed in touch over the following months and years. The Secret Service people were pleasant, kind and down-to-earth. The head of their team was a young man, a recent graduate of the University of Hawaii where he had been a tackle on the football team. At 6'2" and 240 pounds, this gentle giant, Sam Tong, was a fine gentleman. His personality matched his size. Bright eyes and a pleasant grin lit up a room when he entered. His bronze complexion reflected his Hawaiian background. A firm handshake dispelled any question about Sam's authority. This man was sure of himself when he moved about a room. People watched him. He made an impression.

Eight phone lines were temporarily installed. One of those lines was a gift to our staff for having been helpful in the arrangements. We were now able to place calls home routed through the White House exchange, which would cost us nothing. Thank you taxpayers!

Ten days before the big weekend, the Secret Service began reviewing each minute detail relating to the service—doors to be used, windows one would walk past, closets in the area, sharp nails or loose boards. What's in the basement? What's in the attic? They looked at everything. In the rear of the Cathedral was a private alley approximately a hundred yards long and ten yards wide where we could park our cars. A decision was made to direct the President and his party to enter and leave by a back door opening onto this alley. A large tent was constructed so that the Presidential entourage could pass under it and no one from nearby windows would be able to see the occupants of the cars enter or leave. The five cars were armor plated Cadillacs with bulletproof windows. They were baby tanks with five telephones, one for each car.

This rear door entrance entered directly into my office, which in the meantime had been turned into a communications center. I was now spending much of my time going over details with the Secret Service. Every step the President took was discussed. Even on a normal day I had a busy job, but I enjoyed the extra time I now spent on this operation. In fact, I loved it!

It was Thursday, five o'clock in the afternoon before the big Sunday. I was due to be in the center of Paris for a meeting with David McGovern, my Senior Warden. I was tired. I stood up and got ready to leave.

From the window in my office I noticed about twenty burly men in the alley. There was something suspicious happening. I did not understand. I opened the door and asked what was going on? Most of the men were short and stocky and practically all of them were smoking the omnipresent Gauloises. They were the French Secret Service. They didn't ask, but rather demanded, a tour. The head man was not friendly. At this point I didn't feel like being friendly either. "Okay," I said, "but hurry up."

They complained about everything. So I decided to liven this situation up. I showed them the front pew where the Bush family would sit. Then I added that the French President would sit in the third pew. *Mon Dieu*—the boys gasped. No one told us that our President would be here. The twenty Frenchmen all started talking at once. They had heard that their President was *not* going to be at the Cathedral. They left in a hurry to ask more questions about this possibility. I wondered what was going on in their minds. That evening they found out that Mitterrand was indeed not coming and the head of the detail called me. He had a French fit. After a few bad words, he slammed the phone down. I nicknamed him "Inspector Clouseau," after Peter Seller's role in the Blake Edwards' film "The Pink Panther." I found out later that Clouseau was upset, feeling that if Mitterrand were coming he should have been seated in the front pew not the third. *Vive la France.*

On Saturday morning there was a rehearsal with the clergy, choir, and acolytes and a walk-through with the Secret Service. In the evening, Patsy and I had dinner with John Straton, an old friend from New York who was visiting with us. Later we watched a parade on the Champs-Elysees, a five minute walk from the Cathedral. It was the best parade I ever saw in my life. When Jessye Norman stepped out onto an outdoor stage in a blue, white, and red gown symbolizing the French flag, she resembled a majestic ocean liner setting sail. When she started singing *"La Marseillaise"* all of Paris sang with her. My heart skipped several beats. Such a perfect diva!

We went to bed early because the Bomb Squad was arriving at six a.m. to begin their search of the Cathedral and grounds. Three German Shepherd Dogs that could smell explosive materials accompanied them. About 6:30 the next morning, Clouseau arrived unannounced with his group and three more dogs. I was waiting for a dogfight. It was decided that the French team with their three dogs would sniff outside. The American team would take care of the inside. I watched the French dogs, and it seemed that all they wanted to do was pee on our walls. American dogs urinate. French dogs pee. The French gave up once again and left. Snipers arrived and took places on the roofs of nearby apartments on the Avenue, which had been closed early the preceding day to traffic and parked cars. It was an eerie sight to see the Avenue so empty.

At 6:30 in the morning, Patsy made coffee and served croissants from the bakery across the street to the Secret Service, choir members, ushers and others who had to arrive early. Our doors were opened at seven a.m. People were already waiting on the sidewalk. It was required that all enter through a metal detector. No one was to be seated after 8:30 a.m. At that time every seat was assigned and taken.

For the next half hour our choir led us in a hymn sing. I had been a bit unsure if this idea would work, but it turned out to be a smashing success. We sang the old favorites. "A Mighty Fortress is Our God". "Rise Up Ye Men of God". "Lift High the Cross". "Onward Christian Soldiers". We ended with "My Country 'Tis of Thee". The Episcopalians, God's frozen people, were getting warmed up.

At 8:15 Secretaries Brady and Baker and their wives arrived, along with other White House Staff members. The Senior Warden escorted them to their pews. Patsy and I were standing alone in the large Parish Hall to greet the Bushes. My office was too small. The Secret Service brought the Bushes through the office and down to the Hall. It was a moment for the two of us to greet our President and Mrs. Bush. They are outgoing, friendly, warm people. They made us feel comfortable having them in our home. The President asked me about our sons Jonathan and Jason. We walked through the cloister and entered the front doors. Somehow at this point, Pasty and Barbara Bush got ahead of the President and me. The two wives entered the Cathedral ahead of us. I said to the President: "They should follow *us*." He said, "Jim, have you ever tried to tell two Smith women they have to follow? Good luck. I'm not going there!" I agreed. Somehow we eventually got realigned. I led the President and Mrs. Bush, Patsy, and Ambassador Curley and his wife up the center aisle to the first pew.

The congregation was standing. The Cathedral was filled with early morning sun and smiles. Huge pedestals of red and pink roses were on either side of the main altar, which was draped, in a rich white frontal. The historic Cavaille-Coll Organ filled the huge space with glorious sounds. The antiphonal organ in the rear with the trumpet stops combined with the main organ and burst forth with a great Te Deum. What a moment! I returned to the rear, put on my vestments, and gave the signal to our organist to begin the service.

Starting the long walk up the wide center aisle came the large choir, banners, flags, acolytes, and clergy. I was almost afraid to look up from my hymnal because I might "lose my cool." By the time I reached the Dean's stall I had fallen into the rhythm of the service and felt confident. I glanced at the Bushes in the pew. They were wearing big smiles.

I led the President to the lectern where he read the First Lesson. After the Gospel I preached on the theme of freedom. During the Communion service the Peace was exchanged with those in one's pew. At the Recessional I returned to the first pew to escort the five people to the Parish Hall, where we met with the vestry and Parish leaders. When the Bushes entered the Parish Hall the thirty people clapped and cheered. This was another great moment.

I presented the President with a first edition of the French translation of The Book of Common Prayer. He in turn gave me, to my surprise and gratitude, a silver chalice for communion services. I was overwhelmed. We treasure his gift. Then he and Mrs. Bush talked freely for almost an hour with the thirty parishioners invited into the hall. Space was limited so not everyone had a chance to meet the President. Secretaries Brady and Baker and other staff joined in this reception. Secretary Baker thought the freedom sermon was so good he asked for a copy. George Bush said he was having the time of his life. I was "flying high".

I was also tired. I leaned against the twelve-foot high oak doors with heavy wrought iron hinges. It was a good spot to watch and savor the warmth in that reception hall. The doors were closed. No one could enter but soon someone was knocking on the doors. I opened the door a crack and explained that the reception was private.

A man replied: "Gosh I'm always going in places where I wasn't invited."

"What is your name?" I asked.

"Brent Scowcroft," he responded.

"My goodness, man, come in here. You should be here. These are your people."

"Thank you Mr. Dean."

Since that moment I have felt fondness for that humble and unassuming member of George Bush's cabinet.

I shall never forget the departure. Patsy and I led the President's party up the back stairs to the waiting limousines in the alley. In front of the cars were a dozen French motorcycles with flashing lights, a French truck with armed soldiers, three escort cars, and a back-up limo. All of this was waiting in our little back alley. Never before had it seen anything like this.

Sam, our Secret Service friend, got the President and Secretaries Baker and Brady into the lead car. Mrs. Bush and some members of her family left from the front of the Cathedral in another car. Sam shut the car door, and used the radio on his sleeve to whisper in that strange government lingo, "We have a departure." Motorcycles roared, cars' engines revved up and no one could move.

At the entrance to the alley there is heavy steel bar that crosses the width of the alley. It is raised by inserting a pass card in a slot at which time the bar goes up, keeping the alley available only to those with cards. I had given my pass card to a member of the Secret Service earlier that morning so that he could be available to permit the cars to enter and leave when the morning was over. But he had mislaid the card. The enormous steel barrier was down and no one knew how to get it up—no one but me, that is.

I ran to the end of the alley with my cassock flying in the wind. I knelt in front of the control box located at the base of the barrier, pried open the door and faced the by-pass system that will work absent a card. Four buttons must be pushed in the proper sequence. First white, then yellow, then black, then green and only then can the barrier be raised. All was fine so far. The problem facing me was that I always used my card. I had not worked the sequence in years. If the wrong sequence is used, the system takes a few minutes to readjust. Then the entire process must be repeated.

Out of the corner of my eye I could see the crowd across the street laughing and wondering at the delay. The French motorcycle drivers and soldiers were yelling "*Vite, Vite.*" Sam, my Secret Service friend was approaching me at a fast pace. He was not happy. I was sweating bullets. Only God and I knew that I wasn't sure of the sequence. I remembered the first two colors but I wasn't sure of the order of the last two. If I made a mistake we could be here for ten minutes. I hated to see Clouseau in the front seat of the lead car, watching me suffer and enjoying every bit of the suspense. My hands were shaking.

I pushed white and I prayed that Jesus would make this stupid barrier go up. I pushed yellow. I said, "Jesus, if this works I shall never raise my voice at my wife or the children again."

The critical moment was at hand. I was almost sure that the white and the yellow were good; it was the last two that I did not remember. I pushed black. "Jesus if you make this work I won't stare at pretty women. And I'll never again drink too much."

I pushed green, made a hasty confession of my sins and repented for voting for Dukakis. "If this barrier goes up, I'll become a Republican," I promised.

There was moment of silence. I closed my eyes and confessed to God that I had just given in to using black magic theology.

I kept my eyes closed, and then heard the roar of the mechanism across the street. The bar was going up. I was saved. I stood up proud as a peacock. I smiled for the first time, as the newest member of the GOP!

I blew a big kiss to Clouseau. He smiled and waved back. Wow! The President's car passed me. I saluted. He waved back. I felt like having a heart attack.

The agents said goodbye to us and gave us a large photo of the White House, framed and signed by all of them. Sam gave Patsy a kiss. She refused to wash her face for some time after that. Phones disappeared. The tent came down. It became very, very quiet at the American Cathedral on 23 Avenue George V.

We had already packed. An hour later we got into our car. I leaned over and whispered in Pat's ear, "We have a departure," and headed to our favorite beach in Normandy. It was a fantastic weekend.

CHAPTER FOUR

CAFÉ

I begin my mornings at 6:45. It is quiet in the Cathedral. Dim light comes through the Cathedral's remarkable English stained-glass windows casting patterns of multi-colored light across empty pews. Without making a sound, I cross in front of the main altar walking quietly, almost breathlessly, over the stone floors. I enter a small side chapel for my daily ritual, Morning Prayer from my Episcopalian Book of Common Prayer. I feel alive in the rays of light and the atmosphere of silence. Prayer comes naturally to me in this place, at this time, and is one of the joys of living in the American Cathedral in Paris.

Fifteen minutes later I am crossing the avenue in front of the cathedral into a world of noise and confusion. I am headed to my favorite café for coffee and croissant and to read The Herald Tribune. Motorcycles are roaring down the Avenue George V. One can hear them coming from a distance. They are perilous intruders in my world in Paris. Taxis, scooters and cars careen by from opposing directions without slowing, even when an unfortunate pedestrian is caught between the lanes of honking vehicles. I have learned that to be safe, one must cross the avenues only when both lanes are clear of traffic. I make my move and survive to live another day.

Every Frenchman has a favorite café near his home or place of work and in our neighborhood Café George V is a charming oasis. As an adopted Frenchman I, too, love my café. My morning visits have become another kind of morning ritual for me. I know

Monsieur and Madame, the owners of the cafe. I know the waiters, especially Roman who is in his early sixties but passes for seventy. He is always dressed in a black shirt and pants, topped off with a white apron, the upper half rolled to his hefty waist and tied around the back. His bulbous nose reminds me of my grandmother's wooden darning egg once used to repair holes in my socks. The combination of Roman's menacing black eyebrows, bushy and unkempt, and his squat mustache make him look perpetually angry. His frosty sideburns and a wreath-like ruff of white hair that circles his otherwise bald head soften this impression, however. He never smiles. He seldom talks. We know nothing of his personal life, his beliefs, his thoughts. He nods when I enter and when I leave. Roman remains an enigma.

The café's bar is unofficially reserved for men. There men perch at the bar on tall stools or they stand at either end with a foot propped on the brass rail bolted a few inches from the floor. On occasion a pair of secretaries will sit nearby at round linoleum-topped tables with the omnipresent ashtray, and hold whispered conversations.

These early morning patrons have the same routine every day. I affectionately label them "the guests on the Morning Show." They are businessmen, cab drivers, street cleaners, cooks, firemen, lawyers, and assorted others. They are men coming off the night shift and those preparing for the morning shift. Juan, the Spanish bartender, like his clients, never says much. He stands next to the cash register staring into space while slowly shining a glass with a white bar towel, his bent elbow resting on a ledge under the mirror. If you want coffee you raise your cup. If you want another beer or shot of Calvados, you raise your empty glass. One never has to talk during the morning. You nod, point, or raise a glass, and Juan will respond.

There is little conversation. Maybe a complaint about penalty calls against France in last night's soccer game. Or the sorry state of French politics. Everyone seems to shake his head about bad game calls and to acknowledge the political mess in France with another nod or grunt. But much of the time is spent staring into a lengthy mirror that stretches from one end of the bar to the other. One can always look at others without turning his head. One can also stare at one's own reflection in the cloudy and yellowed mirror.

Some people love to do that! During Christmastime this mirror is decorated with pine branches and red plastic balls interspersed with holly and Christmas cards, and despite its tawdriness, all admire this attempt at decoration.

Everybody smokes. The patrons smoke their cigarettes to the bitter end. For the last puff they squeeze the butt between the thumbnail and the tip of the first finger, drawing a deep breath, and at the same time and without a break in the action, discard the smoldering butt into the ashtray, which displays the name of some popular French whiskey. As another cigarette is pulled from the pack sitting in front of them on the bar, the process is begun all over again.

I shall never forget these people I thought of as friends. Though I knew nothing about them, I cherished being among them for those few brief moments every morning for ten years. Every day, as morning gained ground and lunchtime approached, the café became more social and less somber. People smiled and conversed at tables. The café became busy and noisy—more social. But for some strange reason it was the members of the Morning Show whom I loved. I loved watching them smoking, drinking or complaining to no one and everyone about the sorry state of the world and especially of France. Over the years I knew a few of them by name only. I knew little about them. We never said *"bonjour"* or *"au'voir."* I think I envied them. They had a certain freedom. They had concern for neither my shortcomings nor my gifts. They did not judge me. I was accepted at face value. They exhibited the same feeling toward those who sat next to them at the bar every morning, perhaps having never even looked directly into a man's eyes but seeing him only through the dark mirror. How different from my daily life in the Cathedral. I wondered if perhaps the Christian Church could be a little less judgmental and a little more like the Morning Show in the Café George V.

I returned to Paris this past year and noticed that my café had been sold to people who had turned it into a fancy bistro. The long oak bar was now shining chrome with plush bar stools. A gleaming new mirror replaced the smoky one in which we had all regarded one another and ourselves. No black plastic ashtrays. Clean marble tables. Most of all, I felt the absence of the members of the Morning Show, no longer lingering at the bar, nodding, smoking contemplatively, staring into the mirror, sharing their taciturn camaraderie. Something precious was gone now, and I could only feel the sadness of its loss and the poignancy of its memory.

CHAPTER FIVE

MY JOURNEY

I was a reluctant parent when our own adolescent sons were ready to challenge the world like Don Quixote. Their anxieties made me think of my own journey into the world. Many years ago I wanted to grow up in a new space other than school, church or home. I wanted to take charge of myself. The path I chose was not easy for my parents.

My journey began when I was nineteen. By June of 1952, I had graduated from Tabor Academy, a straight-laced New England prep school with a cloistered atmosphere, where my parents had hoped that I would be nurtured and protected. I returned home to Pennsylvania with my belongings and repacked a duffle bag with summer traveling clothes, a camera and two hundred dollars in cash that I had saved during the school year. I went to the train station in Philadelphia, supposedly to catch a train to Norfolk, Virginia. I lied to my parents claiming that I had been invited to visit a girl friend and her parents for a weekend. Instead, I boarded a train to New York City where I took a cab to the Maritime Union hiring hall on Staten Island and signed on as a waiter on a passenger ship.

Four months earlier, while I was still in school, I had paid for a fake I.D. card representing my age as old enough to apply for a Seaman's card. Anyone hoping to work in the U.S. shipping industry needed this card. The process took several weeks and required a form for a physical exam. I filled out an exam form and forged the school doctor's name. I also applied for a passport. My card, passport, and a satisfactory report on my physical exam, arrived a month before graduation. I spent several restless weeks wondering if I would get discovered for this caper.

The Maritime Hall was a huge, dingy place resembling an aircraft hangar. Fifty rusted metal folding chairs sat in a semi-circle in the center of this cavernous room, around a worn brown table the size of a desk. The rest of the building was vacant. The chairs and desk looked lonely in this hollow shell. A bare bulb hung over the table from a long cord wrapped around a beam. A wire basket holding a disorganized mess of papers sat on the table. Next to the basket was a telephone, a relic of bygone days, standing straight up, like an African meerkat on top of his mud home. A removable earpiece hung on a hook, making hearing and speaking separate operations.

A gigantic bare-chested man with mammoth arms and legs and black shiny skin sat and stared at me when I approached the desk. He was reading a comic book. He projected the impression that I was intruding on his privacy, but I needed to add my name to the roster of about thirty applicants sitting behind me.

He did not take his eyes off of me as I handed him the form given to me when I entered the hall. Carelessly, he pushed the paper into the wire box. He raised a fly swatter and gently tapped the bare bulb so that it moved back and forth over his bald head, big forehead, and protruding eyes. What was holding my attention to these lazy moves was that he never took his eyes off of me. I wondered how he knew that the paper would stay in the basket or that the fly swatter would reach the bare bulb. I imagined that perhaps he was a bat in disguise that finds food by echolocation. I was afraid and fascinated by this person I called Bat Man who induced both fear and awe. He was not wearing shoes. The feet belonged to a giant. Special shoe makers must surely have created shoes for this giant. The wide gap between his big toe and the next one would have posed a problem. This man's grotesque feet, I thought, were both fearsome and fascinating.

For two days I stayed around the hangar waiting to be called. When the phone did ring it was usually a request from a ship owner needing electricians, plumbers, or able-bodied seamen. Waiters were at the bottom of the heap. If one wanted to use the men's room or get something to eat one spoke to the man with the comic books. He granted thirty-minute breaks. Disappearance from the hall for additional time moved one to the bottom of the list. At four thirty it was time to leave until eight a.m. the next day. Men went home or stayed with friends for the night. I walked alone to an inexpensive boarding house.

On the second day I was engrossed in a cheap, sexy paperback when I was called. A loudspeaker ordered me to report to the Military Sea Transportation Service ship, General Patch, in three hours. The MSTS shipping line moved Army personnel and their families to foreign ports where our country had military bases. I heaved my duffle bag over my shoulder and moved to the table to receive my written orders. Without a word, Bat Man handed me my papers. I said, "Thank you". He said nothing, but stared at me with his bulbous eyes in a supercilious manner that reminded me of a water buffalo. Whatever friendliness he may have felt toward me seemed sinister and I felt scared.

I called my parents from a pay phone before going to the ship. They had assumed I was in Virginia. There was silence on the other end of the line when I related my story to my mother. Her voice, when she finally spoke, was filled with pain and anger at having been lied to and she urged me to return home.

For a brief second I was hesitant. I closed my eyes and assured her that I was safe and was excited about my summer. I didn't tell her how nervous I was feeling. The brief thought of returning home and forgetting this crazy idea was appealing. I questioned my resolve. But then, I told her not to worry, promised to phone again in a few days, and hung up. I prayed to God I that I was doing the right thing. That phone call was necessary but difficult. I had hurt my parents.

At the gang plank I was assigned a cabin with five other waiters. At twenty feet square, the room resembled a high school gym locker. A long thin bench stretched down the middle. On three sides were three bunk beds, each next to three pairs of wall lockers. A sink with a mirror was attached in a corner. Near the sink and a bulkhead wall was a porthole. The steel walls, floor, and ceiling were painted battleship gray. The room was spotless because of daily inspections. Each one of us took turns making sure our area was clean. A communal bathroom with more sinks, showers and commodes was next to our sleeping unit. On our deck, other crewmembers shared a pattern of units with similar layouts.

Officers had private quarters on upper decks. Enlisted men lived in crowded conditions on lower decks where they slept and ate three meals a day in large mess halls with trays and cafeteria style lines. Kitchen help was drawn from the enlisted ranks. The upper dining rooms for officers had table settings. Meals were served family style three times a day in two different shifts for each meal by thirty waiters like me.

The ship would leave New York City and sail to Bremerhaven, Germany, an eight-day journey.

In the morning we were escorted by tugs to the harbor entrance. I was standing alone on a front deck watching the tugs cut the cords as we gained momentum and the New York coast melted away. I didn't have to report until five p.m. for the first of the two dinner shifts. I was excited. I had died and gone to heaven. I couldn't stand still. I was in a new world. I was alone. I would be seeing things and going places I had dreamed about. I was surrounded by water, the setting sun, and my own dreams.

My life became different from anything it had been before. The gigantic ocean I was seeing seemed to have no beginning, ending, or horizon. I had the sensation of being alone in this world. Like the sea in front of me, there no longer seemed to be horizons or beginnings or endings in my life. No strutting, stuttering schoolmasters. No cheerless chaperones at school dances telling me how to behave. No fun with girls, cigarettes or beer. No intruding parents to complain to strangers and friends about my appearance.

I thought to myself, "Hurry up, General Patch, bring on the world because here comes Jim in a white uniform, carrying a tray, with a serving towel on his arm. Come dance with me, world. I'm ready for you. Alleluia, Lord!" It was a glorious time in my life and I loved this strange new version of myself.

The tugs released this leviathan of a ship. It charged over the rolling blue water and headed for Europe.

The work in the dining hall went on every day at sea. People must eat. Kitchen crews did not get time off. Free time only occurred when we remained in port. Turn around time was usually three days. The ship had to be refurbished. Food and other essentials had to be loaded. Passengers reported when the Patch was ready to sail, and then I would go back to work.

I experienced some good times and some bad moments on board. There were twenty four of us to take care of the tables. Twenty-three of the men were either Puerto Rican or African-American. I was the youngest and the only Caucasian. The captain's dinner was held on the last evening of each trip. The dessert for this meal was always flaming baked Alaska.

Lights are dimmed. A pianist plays a military march. Twenty-three of us walk in step through the dining room with flaming Alaskas on our tray. I was last hired. I am the youngest. I enter last. I am white. I appear, the applause stops, there is a nervous laugh. I am out of place. The Southern officers and others of their mindset complain that I should not be in this lineup.

Not only in the dining room, but in other places, I always felt an awkward pressure. In the hallways, I hugged the walls. If I walked down the middle of the hall, I got pushed aside. It seemed that wherever I went, I was excluded. I was all too white. The others were too dark. They were many. I was one. The African-Americans, Puerto Ricans and white men formed separate groups. I was isolated by my job and in my living quarters. I had to live with the dark side of life on the General Patch.

In the movies during the evenings after work, I sat apart. Everyone brought a chair from his room to watch the show. During one of these evenings, I left for the bathroom and returned to find my chair gone. I retreated to my bunk. I suffered in silence. I could do nothing. I had never suffered rejection like this before.

Thirteen years later, when I was curate in a church in Larchmont New York, I participated in the Selma—Montgomery march in Alabama with Martin Luther King because I knew first hand the misery, loneliness, and sin of racism.

On the return trip to New York I decided to leave this job. In another seven days I would be free. On the last evening I heard a kind word from one of my bunkmates. I was delirious with joy and decided to stay on. I did not want these feelings of rejection to drive me away. I needed to learn to handle this problem. That kind word from a Puerto Rican bunkmate helped me grow up.

On the next trip, after making the turnaround in New York, we headed South through the Panama Canal stopping briefly in Hawaii for twenty four hours to take on supplies and more personnel before heading for Yokahama, Japan. In Hawaii I stayed up all night and slept on the beach after a large party. I had to be back at the ship by 5:30 the next morning. Nursing a hangover, I started walking the two miles. There was no one on the streets or sidewalks. Honolulu was asleep. Walking seemed to help clear my head. In front of me was a row of parking meters. I decided to leap frog as many as I could to see if I could reach the next intersection. I did not hear the police car come up behind me and sound his siren. I had to stop and show him my pass from the ship. He made me get into the car. I thought I was getting a break from a kind policeman giving me a ride to the ship.

Not so! I was taken to a police station and arrested for disturbing the peace. I was booked and fined thirty five dollars. A door was opened at the end of the room. I entered and was led to a large holding pen containing fifty four ship mates of the General Patch. They had been picked up earlier for fighting in a bar with G.I.s. When they saw me they were all smiles—I had become accepted! They even clapped when I was led into the cell. It was if we were war comrades who had faced the enemy and fought like heroes. I never mentioned my battle with the parking meters of Honolulu. We were placed in a bus with bars on the windows and taken directly to the ship with police escort cars in front and rear. Honolulu never wanted to see us again and informed the Captain of that news. From this hangover morning I had become accepted as one of them. I was happy. A turning point had been reached.

The turnaround point from Yokohama was Seattle, Washington. I disembarked and headed back home to attend college in September. To save money I hitch-hiked as far as Chicago and took the train to Philadelphia. My parents were dumbstruck when they saw me. At first they were angry but when I told them some of my experiences and how many places I saw and how much money I had been able to save, they calmed down. In June, after my first year of college, I returned to Staten Island and signed on again as waiter for another summer with MSTS.

In her book, *Coming of Age in Samoa*, Margaret Meade explains how the maturation process takes place. When a teenager reaches a certain age, he is sent into the jungle to face the fears and dangers of a wild and separate place. At the end of the week the young man returns home to his hut in the village with a cup of clean, clear water. His mother is waiting at the entrance to the hut and holds a bowl to receive the water. Her son throws the water in his mother's face, signifying his new independence. This ritual signifies the entrance into adulthood, and so, in my own way, had I made my own entrance.

CHAPTER SIX

A FAMILY TRIP TO SPAIN

The day before a vacation is an exciting time at the Deanery. Patsy, Jonathan, Jason and I are off tomorrow to Spain for a month. The car was returned yesterday after a maintenance check. We are packing clothes, cameras, and guidebooks. The boys are taking obscure miscellaneous items, which have nothing to do with a month in Spain. Tomorrow I shall practice triage on duffle bags and back packs they have filled.

Patsy is in charge of tour books, Parador locations, and maps in places we will visit. She earmarks points of interest such as cathedrals, museums, monasteries, castles, and beaches. Her plans are flawless.

The excitement takes a downhill turn. The boys are arguing and calling each other four letter words. Patsy is complaining about the mess in the house. The three men in the Leo household live with a neatnik. I once complained that if I went to the bathroom in the middle of the night I would return to find my bed made. I want to disappear to my cafe across the street to read the Herald Tribune.

Emotions soon return to normal and the fighting ceases. Was this just another storm in a teacup? Or were larger issues involved?

For most of their early years, our sons were raised in the parsonage in Tuxedo Park, New York. Tuxedo Park is a private community developed by a group of wealthy New Yorkers at the end of the 19th century as an exclusive weekend retreat. The carefully chosen members of Tuxedo Park had built large mansions surrounding three lakes. A private clubhouse, golf course, and Episcopal Church were added as part of the community. As years passed, the mansions were transformed into permanent residences and a grade school from first through eighth grade was added. After completing ninth grade, students were customarily sent to boarding school for their final four years before college.

Tuxedo Park has not changed dramatically since its founding. High walls still surround the park. A large entrance gate protects the inhabitants from unwanted visitors or sightseers. Our sons felt that the walls and gate, while symbols of exclusiveness for some, were signs of restriction and prohibition for them. The parsonage, moreover, was a fishbowl. Parishioners wanted to know about our sons and their activities, especially when trouble was involved. It was all fodder for gossip.

We had moved to France in the middle of a school year, where I would serve as rector of the American Cathedral in Paris. In order to finish ninth grade at the local school before coming to Paris and attending a French bilingual school, our younger son Jason stayed behind in New York with a classmate whose parents lived in our parish in Tuxedo Park.

Earlier in the week the boys had made an effort to be permitted to remain in Paris for the month. They complained that being with the two of us in a car, in hotel rooms, and sharing three meals a day for almost a month was family-time overload. They wanted stay in Paris while we went to Spain. While I understood firsthand their desire to find some space between themselves, the church, and their parents, I hoped our boys would stay in a safe place of love and care. I didn't want them venturing out in the modern world full of drugs, alcohol and sex, but understood that their own search for meaning and maturity involved taking risks. I was reluctant to practice what I preached in matters of maturation and independence.

But more importantly, there were reasons why we had to leave Paris for a month as a family. First, of course, I was excited about being together. Jonathan had been attending St. George's School in Newport, Rhode Island, returning to Paris only on school vacations. We had not spent much time as a family in recent years. Secondly, we were literally moving out of Paris for the month, leaving our home and the Cathedral in the charge of an experienced priest during our absence. The Most Reverend Frank Griswold, the Presiding Bishop of our National Church, with his wife and two daughters, would live in the Deanery and take services on Sundays. The boys had to come with us. Their house in Paris was no longer available.

It was good for me to leave the problems at the Cathedral. I was tired. I needed a break. Every parish has problem parishioners—others have problem rectors. In the U.S. there is usually another Episcopal church in the area and unhappy people can move to new places and begin new lives. Not so in Paris. The nearest Episcopal Church was in Belgium. We had to live together in Paris with our problems. I left confident that the Cathedral was in good hands. Parishioners would enjoy the Griswold family and the few spoilers would calm down and, with me out of the way, act civilly.

There was the subject of finances. Touring in Europe with four people is expensive. I had looked forward to our trip and begun saving earlier in the year. Reservations had been made ahead of time in Paradors, those historic castles, monasteries and ancient fortresses restored over time by the Spanish government into overnight stopovers for tourists. The food was always good. The rooms were clean. Best of all, an overnight stay was reasonably priced. I owned a car so we did not have a rental expense but buying gas in Europe is expensive. Tolls on the auto routes are numerous and costly. But with our savings and Patsy's meticulous planning, as careful and well thought out as her management of the home, our trip was to become a reality.

Early the next morning, the four Leos left Paris together and headed south. I was leaving the difficult parishioners at the Cathedral altar. I could not imagine giving up this time in our life together. I was flying high.

I sped down the auto route in our VW station wagon heading for Spain. We were a happy group. The boys had on earplugs for listening to tunes on their Walkmans. They seemed to have gotten over their angst about being together for a month. I promised them I would be sensitive to their feelings of confinement and restriction. Glancing in the rear view mirror I could see them moving their hands and bodies in rhythm with what they referred to as music. Pats was enjoying shuffling maps and papers and organizing a picnic lunch for her brood.

I then introduced my great idea. We would be returning home at the end of the month on the same day as everyone else. The month of August remains a traditional vacation month in Europe.

It is a huge migration. Summer vacations are over at the end of August. *La rentree* in Europe is similar to Labor Day in the United States. Roads are packed. Motels and hotels are filled. On this day Europe is on the move.

I calculated that if we left our summer rental in Malaga, Spain at 7:30 a.m. on the day before *la rentree*, we would arrive at a place closer to Paris at around 4:00 p.m. and we could avoid the rush and crowds on the following day. On the map I located a town near this point on the auto route. Two days later as I drove through the town, I spotted a hotel. I left the others to wait in the car while I ran inside and hastily reserved two adjacent rooms, for the night at the end of the month. I ignored my sense that the place was not a high quality establishment, considering only that we were staying for just one night and the price was cheap.

For the next three weeks we visited historic cities. We toured ancient castles. We ventured into age-old monasteries, and read about the history of Spain. Some of our time was spent in a beachfront condo on the beach in Malaga graciously lent to us by good friends in Paris and we lounged in the sun with other tourists. From Malaga we managed day trips inland to see the genuine Spanish Spain, away from tourists seeking sun on the beach. Our VW took us to small villages and towns. We ate their food and heard their music. We saw farms and rundown shacks where people lived. We saw stone ruins of bygone ages in the middle of wheat fields.

We watched every day as life and existence came to a halt at one p.m. Streets emptied. Shutters banged closed. Activity stopped. Vendors in the open air markets spread large plastic sheets over fresh produce on their stands. Mangy dogs belonging to no one found shade under houses or nearby trees. Skinny feral cats crept under beat up trucks and carts to sleep in the orange dust. It was siesta time in Spain. On Sunday, villages all over this country were stricken with sleep. It was the end of the world. One of these Sundays, we found a small cafe open for lunch and drank Spanish beer and ate paella by ourselves. Siesta time changes the universe for Spaniards.

There is one celebration occurring every day in Spain. One rises in the late morning to indulge in long crispy pieces of sugary fried dough called churros. My mouth thanked me every morning when I walked into a churreia for hot chocolate and churros. When I remember these mornings, I taste Spain.

On one memorable evening, the boys had gone off on their own while Patsy and I found ourselves at a flamenco bar in Seville. The drama of that dance and music made for an evening never to be forgotten.

It had been a time of new experiences. We realized that this would be the last summer the four of us could take a trip as a family for this length of time. Both of the boys would need to get paying jobs for the following summer to help with education expenses. Jason would be a counselor in a boys' camp in Maine. Jonathan would sign on as a crewman on a Maxi boat, a racing sailboat, and speed across the Atlantic Ocean to compete with other Maxi boats in the Mediterranean. But for now, Jason was to return to a French school on Monday. Jonathan would stay with us until the end of the week before returning to St. George's School in Rhode Island to complete his senior year. On the following day, we would begin our return trip to Paris to start the fall season.

We left our condo in Malaga at around 7:00 a.m. as planned. The boys were exhausted because they had been to an all-night disco the night before. They would sleep in the car. We were to have a morning of peace and quiet on the road. Late in the afternoon we spotted our evening's lodgings in the distance. I pulled into the parking lot and took out a single bag, which contained our dopp kits and changes of clothes. Our funds were almost depleted.

Across the road was an inexpensive restaurant where we could have dinner. Our hotel, upon closer inspection, was clearly tawdry but I pointed out that it didn't matter since we were only staying one night and it was cheap. The cash was down to a trickle. Taking four people on this month's tour in Europe was just as costly as we had anticipated.

We obtained our keys and went to our adjoining rooms. I could tell that Pats was not happy with the accommodations I had so hastily selected a month earlier. The beds were iron cots with skimpy mattresses. A linoleum floor was stained and dull. Tiles were cracked and had missing pieces. A tiny, dim lamp sat on a plastic bedside table with a plastic ashtray. There were no private bathrooms, only public bathrooms down the hall. The place resembled a county jail. There was no air conditioning. It was warmer outside than in, so we kept the windows closed. Already, it was a nightmare. We flopped on our beds. Patsy wasn't talking. She stared into space. I was afraid to say anything. It had been a hard drive with lots of traffic. Tempers were short.

Jonathan and Jason came pounding on our door yelling for us to open up and let them in the room. The worst was yet to come.

"Mom and Dad, peek out the door! Half naked men and women are running up and down the hall!"

The boys were right. This was not a tourist lodging at all, but one of those seamy establishments that we would notice, from time to time, that let out rooms and beds by the hour for activities of a "casual" nature. Patsy was speechless. She quietly told the boys to get their clothes and mattresses and bring them into our room. She turned to me at first without saying a word.

Then she upbraided me for having brought them all to such a place, for bringing to pass all her mother's predictions and warnings about me, for abandoning my responsibilities as a clergy, for being a negligent parent. She suggested that I sleep on the floor myself. I tried to explain that three weeks ago when I stopped here I did not bother to look at rooms and never dreamed it was one of many such places on this route. How was I to know?

The building was U shaped. We were located on one side of this building, with a similar wing opposite to ours. We could look out our window and see into the rooms in the other wing. This new opportunity quickly caught the attention of the boys. I tried to move their mattresses to a place in the room where they could not see the amorous activities taking place a few yards away. To my recollection, none of the windows had shades, neither ours nor those of the occupants across the way.

There was no use trying to find another hotel with a vacancy. We would have to stay here for the night. We tried to sleep. The boys thought this was a world-class experience and kept whispering and giggling. Patsy wasn't talking to me. I kept silent and pretended I was asleep.

At 6:00 a.m. I woke everyone to announce that we were leaving. I wanted out of this place with iron cots, the smell of Lysol, dirty floors and public bathrooms.

On the trip home there were opportunities to talk about our August trip. The only thing the boys wanted to discuss was this last night. My concern was that this accident would get around the congregation at breakneck speed. I knew that there were those in the congregation who would relish this scandal and the opportunity to capitalize on it.

Later in the day we began to talk about other times in Spain and life returned to normal. Pats resumed her more customary, sunny nature and the boys were arguing in the back seat once more. I began to feel good. I had wonderful memories with the friendliest people I know. The Spaniards' love of life seemed contagious. Once again, I felt the blessing of having been able to take one more trip with our family, traveling to foreign countries, seeing and associating with people of different looks, likes and dislikes, and accumulating common memories of good times and bad that would bind our family together through future times. I looked forward to returning to our home in Paris and felt a renewed confidence that I could handle the challenges before me.

CHAPTER SEVEN

STARTING IN HARTFORD

In the spring of 1960 I moved to Hartford, Connecticut to enter a training program at a large insurance company. Twenty-three other college graduates my age were enrolled in this program as well. By this time, I had already graduated from Bucknell University and spent two years in the US Army. I had worked in one of my stepfather's printing companies but felt I was treading water and needed to think of something more fulfilling for myself than working in the printing industry and living at home.

June and July in Hartford that summer were hot and humid. Thinking back on it now, I feel the heat. I smell it. I can taste it. I can see it. A thermometer in the window of a hardware store reads ninety-eight degrees. I am bored and hot. I am beginning to believe that Hartford does not have a soul. Boston has a soul. Philadelphia has a soul. New York City does not have a soul but it has lots of "other stuff." Hartford, Connecticut does not have a soul and it does not have lots of "other stuff."

With Benjamin, another member of the training program, I had rented a third floor studio near Trinity College. It was as ugly as it was cheap and dirty, and Ben was as messy as I. There were four windows but only two screens. No air conditioning. A ceiling fan with paddles that looked like baby elephant ears was grinding in slow painful circles under a ceiling marked with graffiti by our predecessors. Three plastic Christmas tree balls hung over the three paddles and tinsel was looped over all. The fan made more noise than air.

We moved in on a Friday afternoon. By six o' clock our small room with its two iron cots, two lumpy mattresses and bath with a stained tub and sink, had become our home. Beer cans, used boxes, and crumpled newspaper lay strewn on the floor. The toilet resembled one I saw in a dilapidated Caribbean airport. Black and white tiles on the floor were faded, with pieces missing or chipped. The odor was permanent. The door could never stay closed.

Scattered on the floor of the main room and stuck on furniture and our clothing were shredded strips of newspaper for packing breakable things in boxes. Try to pick them up and they stick to your hands. Try sweeping them up, and they stick to the broom.

Rock and roll tunes blasted from an RCA plastic radio with missing knobs and a metal coat hanger jammed into a hole in the top for an aerial. Empty beer cans thrown around the room seemed to improve the sound. The more we drank, the better the music. Our other big purchase had been a second hand portable TV from a rummage sale in the First Baptist Church a block away.

Ben and I celebrated our new friendship and the start of our career with this large life insurance company. Flopping on beds amidst the scattered shreds of paper, we opened two beers. Shaking the cans we sprayed suds on the floor to baptize our palace. Bill Haley and the Comets were playing loud and clear on our plastic radio. We were flying high.

On this hot Friday afternoon, we walked three blocks to an outdoor café where throngs of young people from nearby offices were celebrating the week's end and their upwardly mobile aspirations. Most were graduates of different colleges and enrolled in training programs in Hartford. We were anxious to inform them, especially the young ladies, of our sure and certain advancement into the world of higher finance and big business.

*   *   *

Eight weeks later I was going nuts. At this point I was beginning to wonder if I had strayed into another employment disaster. Would I ever make it through this short unhappy life? First, a bust in the printing business and now questions about the insurance game. I enjoyed the other trainees in our weekly meetings, but I could not explain why I had been selected. I would lie awake at night and stare at our elephant eared fan with tinsel and Christmas tree balls. I was feeling crummy, like our room. I wanted to get out of this apartment, the insurance company and Hartford. The question was, could I do it gracefully? I wanted a responsible excuse for saying no, no, no.

Weekly meetings with our group seldom produced anything interesting or challenging. We were informed that on the following Monday at nine 'o clock in the morning, the president of the company would talk to us about our future with the company. I had hoped that this might reassure me. Our CEO was rumored to be the Second Coming. We were told to be here and be on time. No excuses. This is Show Time my little children. Miss this one and you can say goodbye. I started to think about this last thought.

At 8:45 a.m. Monday, I was walking to work. The streets and sidewalks of Hartford were clean. This city appeared antiseptic and boring. Nobody dared to jaywalk, litter, or spit in the gutters. Women wore dresses down to the knees. Stockings with seams went straight up the backs. They kept their eyes straight ahead. No flirting on the highways of Hartford. Many were chewing gum and I wondered where they would spit it out. Men wore gray business suits and Panama hats and were carrying leather brief cases. I think now of our astronauts marching to their space rockets carrying suitcases and looking alike in silver suits and space helmets. Maybe Hartford inspired NASA.

At 8:55, we were seated. Folded hands placed on the tables. We stared ahead with blank looks. Silence in the room was heavy. No one was talking. I wondered if we were breathing. A large podium with a microphone bent to the center by a flexible tube sat on a small raised platform near our chairs. The room, like the silence, was oppressive. I wondered why the mike. I soon learned why.

At 9:00 a.m. the clock struck. The door opened. Mr. Big strode in. He looked mighty. I was impressed. Here was a man who gets his own way. No one holds him back. The light is always green for Mr. Big. He scared me. My impression was that he was 285 pounds and 6'10". Droopy jowls led me to guess that behind that silk gray suit were rolls of fat. Dark gray hair flattened onto his head and parted in the middle was the same color as the suit, with the same reflective quality. This look had to be planned.

Then Big's impression took two hits. I was sitting on a chair at the end of a row. When he came through the door I thought an elephant had entered the room. Then I noticed that he was walking on a two foot wide raised runway across the stage. Reaching the podium he stepped upon a raised box. Mr. Big was not big. He was maybe 5'5, but still plenty fat. He became Mr. Small. But the next hit was devastating. From my chair at the end of the row I had a side view of all the man from head to toe standing behind the podium. I saw his reflecting suit, his black shoes—and then the shocker! Big was wearing white socks.

He began. I then knew the reason for the mike. The walls, the ceiling, the floor, under the table, behind the curtains, maybe even the streets of Hartford were echoing his voice. He began with the history of the company in a fast pace, never slowing down. We learned in less than a minute the hundred and some years of the greatest company in the world. We who were sitting ducks in front of him were now part of this family. We would be taken care of and nurtured. We would be rewarded with good livings and stability and respect in the community if we gave our lives to this great enterprise.

Now the hook! We must give our hopes, our dreams, our daily lives, our weekends, and our hearts to Life Insurance. Make this pledge and our lives would change. My mind was going in circles. Mr. Big, now Mr. Small, in his reflecting gray suit, black shoes, and tacky white socks was bombarding me to give my life away to an almighty God called Life Insurance.

Then it happened. I cringe when I remember this moment. I should have quietly left after the speech. But I didn't. This was the beginning of an important day in my life.

I stood up and announced that I shall never give my life to this company. I was leaving here and attending seminary in September. I was giving my life to Jesus Christ. I turned and walked to the door in the back of the room. Mr. Big's big voice followed me yelling at our mentor to make sure the door didn't hit me in the ass on the way out. I was fired with enthusiasm.

Once on the street I felt good for a few minutes. I didn't like Hartford. I didn't like the insurance business, but reality soon set in. What was I going to do? I had not thought about going to seminary for years. In college I considered a vocation with the church but was more interested in riotous living. My bombshell that July morning was as surprising to me as it was to everybody else in the room. Prayer was not an active part of my life. I had not prayed for anything in recent memory.

Feelings of freedom turned to fear and embarrassment. "Oh God, what have I done with my life?!"

*   *   *

The route back to the apartment passed Trinity College Chapel. A stupendous gothic edifice dressed in pristine white marble, it was and remains today one of the Episcopal Church's most majestic places of worship.

The chapel was empty. It was good to be alone. Most of the students and faculty had left for the summer months. Dorms were empty, except for some involved in summer conferences. Cars seemed to move slowly. Birds softly warbled their love calls. Yardmen sitting on rider mowers moved at a snail's pace. Mother Nature was relaxing after working hard in April and May to produce flowers and cover her trees with pink and white blossoms, which had now been replaced by dark green leaves. The campus was at rest preparing for the fall season. It was a pleasant place.

I found a seat in the second pew up front in order to be close to the altar and the cross. Being stuck for words, it helped to stare at the cross.

I searched for a suitable prayer by scanning The Book of Common Prayer. This didn't work. Opening a Bible, I tried one of those things that some people do when they are in trouble. They close their eyes and open to any page, hoping for some direction in a text on that selected page. I opened to the page that told the story of Jesus turning water into wine. The last thing I wanted or needed was a bottle of home made wine. Trying the same trick with the Hymnal I opened to "Silent night". All was neither calm nor bright that July morning.

I started to worry about the many problems that were sitting in my lap. I needed a job. I had enough cash to last three weeks. I had to make a call to my parents. They weren't about to slay a fatted calf or have a feast when their Prodigal Son appeared on the front steps.

5:00 pm. The chapel would be closing. I would have to abandon my hideout. I spoke to God: "If you are there and can hear me, I wish you would speak up. I am thirsty, hungry and hurting. I have wrecked myself. God, if you are there—if you exist—then do something!"

The sexton, locking the doors as he passed through, walked across the transept and stopped by my shoulder.

"You have been here all day. Are you all right? Can I be any help?"

The sexton turned out to be The Rev. Moulton Thomas, the college Chaplain. When he looked at my face he knew I was in trouble. Tears were forming. Without waiting for a response he led me to a reception room.

There was a library table, dark mahogany with a beautiful French finish, at one end, surrounded by six matching chairs. A stone fireplace with huge andirons. The fireplace was high enough for me to walk into without hitting my head. Walls were book lined. Heavy blue velvet curtains stood guard at high windows. Five wall sconces would probably give the room a warm glow on a cold evening. This place was meant to be used in the winter. On this July evening it felt to me a formidable refuge and a place of safety.

A Presbyterian pastor, a friend of the Chaplain, was seated by the fireplace. I was introduced and sat down. The three of us pulled our chairs close and the Chaplain said a prayer. I knew I was in a safe place.

"Talk to us, James", Reverend Thomas said.

6 p.m. I didn't need encouragement. I wanted to talk. I wanted to tell someone what I had done. I had reached a point where I wanted sympathy. I wanted forgiveness for my past. I could have talked for a week. I started with the scene that morning at the insurance company. I couldn't get it out fast enough. Time seemed to stop.

I talked about my past and exaggerated my sins and failures. I did not like myself! Shame was on my mind. I had let too many people down. My new friends were patient. They didn't say anything. They listened. I was on a run. I indicated that maybe, just maybe, I wanted to be a priest. I asked them to say something to me that made sense.

For the next half hour the Chaplain and his friend talked slowly and without interruption speaking back and forth in slow muted tones. The only sounds in the world were the soft voices of these two men. I was listening to every word.

"James, being a clergyman takes commitment that few can live with. One's life in the church comes before any thing else. One's family, friends, hopes for wealth, and secular achievements mean less. One's past is over. It is forgiven. One becomes a new man in Christ. One's life now is no longer one's own. One belongs to God. One will become the hands of Christ", explained the Chaplain.

I thought briefly about Mr. Big and his similar words on this subject. I remembered that I also said earlier in the day that I wanted to be a priest. Twice in one day I had said something I wasn't sure I believed. The Chaplain said you have to give your life God. Mr. Big said you must give your life to the Insurance God in Hartford. There was a world of difference.

The Presbyterian minister had been somewhat quiet up to this point. Now he talked about his calling and what the life of a clergyman meant to him. The idea of commitment was coming through loud and clear. We then prayed together, seeking God's forgiveness and thanking him for the gifts we have to offer.

The Chaplain prayed for me and prayed that the Holy Spirit would guide and protect me in the months and years to come.

My tears flowed. I had not openly wept for years. On that evening my hopes, my tears, my joy, came together. I was a whole person. I was a new person. I gave my life to Christ. We arose together. I thanked them for giving me a new hope for the future. I didn't want to leave. They realized their job on this evening with me was over. It was time for me to be alone. Leaving me then was a wise thing to do.

I felt light headed. At that moment, my life was changing. In an instant, I loved my God whom I didn't understand and I loved myself whom I didn't understand either. I knew that God in Jesus Christ loved me in a way I never thought possible. I was a new person. God did answer my prayer by sending two men to listen and talk to me about life lived in the Christian faith. I sit here almost fifty years later and recall that day at Trinity College and I am thankful for that early evening at the Trinity Church Chapel.

On the way home from the chapel I knew I must face Ben who is a wild cynic. I had some cold feet. He would never understand. I opened our door, which never had a key. Ben was seated on the couch drinking a "Bud" and watching a quiz show. Without looking at me, he asked, "Are you nuts?"

"Ben, please be quiet and listen. I don't know why I said what I said this morning. I can't explain it". I was embarrassed.

Ben continued to watch the game show. He would not look at me. He was upset and probably angry.

I began with my time in the chapel, alone and praying for guidance. I told him how my prayers had risen to the ceiling and dropped back to land dead on the floor. I explained how the Chaplain had arrived at the end of the day and asked me to come with him to a room in a small wing off to the side of the chapel.

"What was the room like?" Again, not looking at me but watching the quiz show.

I described the room and the safety I had felt in that place. I told how the three of us had sat on chairs by the mammoth fireplace and how the chaplain had encouraged us to draw our chairs closer and had said a brief prayer.

I told Ben everything about the day from the beginning to the end. I spoke of how I had spilled out my thoughts, hopes and desires to these two—my shame, my sense of failure. That I told them I had considered becoming a priest and how they had expressed their own feelings about being clergymen. How they had emphasized the importance of giving one's life to Jesus and living a life for others. How our goal should never be the "common gold." How we had knelt in front of our chairs and joined hands.

I told Ben how I had walked home on the air, feeling alive and well. And finally, how I had looked forward with hesitation to talking to Ben, one of my favorite cynics.

Ben said nothing. Now, he was looking at me. Standing up, he left the TV, reached into the ice chest and opened two cans of beer. He walked to where I was standing. I was vulnerable. Ben handed me a beer, and gave me a big hug. I even noticed a smile. I breathed again! I felt tears coming for the third time that day.

"Go get 'em big boy. You are the man." I felt huge affection for Ben. He was the first person to hear my story and give me encouragement.

That evening in Hartford I joined a community of believers who had found a deep faith, not the kind found only on Sunday mornings at eleven a.m. When I left the chapel I changed my mind about many things. Hartford now had a soul. To this day whenever I pass through Hartford on the Connecticut Turnpike, I offer a prayer of thanksgiving for the city.

Also, I have purchased life insurance polices for myself and the rest of the family.

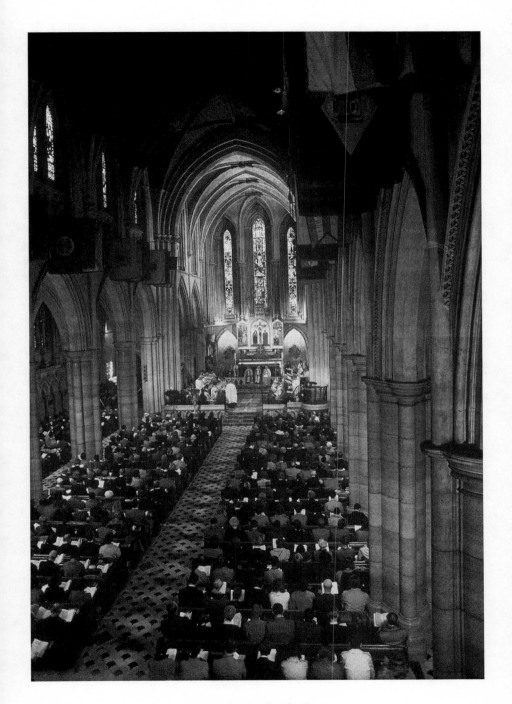

Paris Cathedral

Tourist Barge, (Bateau Mouche)

Choir at Christmas Paris Cathedral

Four good friends. Shelby and Gale Davis with Patsy and Jim

Christ Church Cathedral

CHAPTER EIGHT

CONVERSION

In the days, and weeks, and years to come I would recall that July evening in Hartford, Connecticut when I had arrived at the Trinity College chapel broken and distraught, and been rescued. This type of experience never exactly repeated itself except in my memory. That huge moment years ago invited me to make an about-face in my life. Then I had wanted to take first steps. Today, almost fifty years later, I find a faith expressed in the Church community and through the words of the liturgy. I love to talk with people about the faith.

Over the years I have had thoughts about my experience. I believe the Holy Spirit is inside of everyone. There was no outer invasion of my life. No one dropped in from outer space. The experience was within me, arising from something inside of me. I knew I was a child of God. I knew I was loved. Words at this point become imprecise. How does one talk about love? When I try to talk about God, I fall short.

Soren Kierkegaard, the 19th century Danish philosopher and theologian, talks about a leap of faith as opposed to faith founded in reason. Kierkegaard denies any possibility of doctrinal truth leading one to the faith. He often stated that, "truth is subjectivity."

For me, the conversion experience was instantaneous. For most people in the congregations I served, religious belief has been formed over time and a life of growing up in the Christian faith. I feel that I have to be careful about explaining my experience. My listeners have probably not had momentous earth shaking experiences of this kind. Would I make them feel less Christian because they had not received such a conversion? Christianity is essentially a humbling and unifying thing.

I remind myself and others that this experience took place within a Christian community. There were two other people in that room in Hartford that spring night. St. Paul advises others in the Church to recognize that God works in different ways with different people. St. Paul believes the knowledge of Christianity is not a solitary or personal possession. One's personal knowledge of Christ is something he possesses as a member of the Christian community. Personal experiences such as Paul's conversion on the road to Damascus can sometimes tend to separate the person from other believers.

Instant conversion experiences are not new to the religious world. Millions of people through all ages have undergone this experience. In the First Century, a Jew named Saul had a conversion on the Damascus road. He then became known as Paul. Sometime in the 4th Century St. Augustine surrendered his life to Jesus while sitting in an apple orchard reading a book. Francis, in the Middle Ages, gave up a life of privilege and wealth to minister to the people of God as a simple friar.

Men and women and teenagers. Bankers on Wall Street. Passengers on airplanes. People in hospital waiting rooms. A lone soldier in a firefight in Baghdad. Those at graduations from colleges, medical schools, and law schools. Participants in Billy Graham Crusades. A freshman alone in a dorm room at University. A young woman from Cincinnati giving thanks for recovering from breast cancer at the age of 25. These people had come to the end of their ropes, like millions before them. They turned to God because they were hurting. God answered them in a dramatic and exciting moment. The surest way people approach the Cross is by a beast called suffering. Some have said Christianity is a crutch. They may be right but I have never met a person who is not limping.

Once in a while someone, usually a charismatic Christian, will ask me if I have been "saved". I say yes, I was saved at three o' clock in the afternoon two thousand years ago on a hill called Calvary. When I point this out, this conversation must take place within the right atmosphere. That atmosphere begins with God. God did something to me on that June night in Hartford. I received a gift I didn't deserve. My life was started again by receiving a gift of grace. So, was I born again? Yes, again and again and again. On so many occasions my journey has not been easy or smooth. I have faltered, been stopped, and deterred, but wherever I am, I know I can start again. So in a sense I can be born again. Christianity's diamond is that we are forgiven and can start again.

How do we do this? There are many gods in our society today. Who are we going to serve? The prophets enjoined the Jews to give up the worship of Baal and return to the God of Israel who made a covenant with his people. Like the early Jews, we in the 21st century are faced with choices every day. Like those early Jews, we are faced with the choices of worshipping false gods.

In my position I have often spoken with people who were hurt by the institutional church. They ask: "Can I return?" They have been in the far country for too long. I try to reassure them that they can always come back. Our God is a loving God. You will always be accepted. Not only individuals, but the church itself, has to born again, and again, and again. Being born again is a way of life. It is the Church's job to be born again.

CHAPTER NINE

LEAVING PARIS

In the spring of 1990 I flew from Paris to New York City for a national meeting of the Episcopal Church, and during that time had an opportunity to meet members of the Christ Church search committee. They had come to New York from Cincinnati, Ohio for an interview with me. They were looking for a new priest to be the head of their clerical team and a member of Christ Church had submitted my name to them.

I was impressed with the group's openness to the problems and challenges facing Christ Church and the city of Cincinnati. This interview was frank, open, and honest. I had good feelings about their parish and believed that they felt comfortable with my own questions and answers. When I returned to Paris I mailed them my resume and waited to hear from them.

I, too, had much to consider. Up to that point in my career, I had served in five churches. It was always challenging to face opportunities to minister in a new parish. The work of directing the American Cathedral in Paris was not too different from the work in parishes in the States. The work of prayer was always at the top of the list. In addition to the major service on Sundays, there were weekly services for study groups. American students studying in Paris for a year had a weekly service followed by a dinner and fellowship. There were healing services for those seeking comfort from illness. Marriage blessings, study groups, weddings and funerals, choir rehearsals and concerts all took time and required direction.

Now I needed to think about the realities of leaving Paris. In Paris, administration took place in offices adjacent to the Cathedral where each Canon and some laypeople had private offices. This work involved matters related to maintaining the building, paying the bills and recording the income. Compliance with red tape created by the French bureaucracy was always a challenge. Security was a serious issue since American interests in Paris were often threatened. Hiring security personnel was expensive. Someone placing a bomb in the church was a possibility. We had not formerly encountered this kind of thinking. This was a responsibility that we did not have in common with our counterparts in the States who were not subject to the need for this degree of security.

Most significantly, leaving my position at the American Cathedral would mean leaving a place where my wife Patsy, our two sons, and I had had unforgettable moments. My departure would mean leaving a favorite cafe, lunchtimes on the Bateaux-Mouches, a world of music, art, drama, food, wines, travel to other countries, and loving friends.

Moments in Paris came flooding over me: In my vision of Paris, sidewalk cafés overflow with people. It is lunchtime on a sunny Tuesday in May. A musician strums a guitar. A gypsy with dark eyes and a flashing smile plays soulful melodies on an accordion. He wears a white ruffled shirt, his waist circled by a bright red sash. A monkey wearing a red and black top hat secured by a thin strap under his chin sits on the man's shoulder. The monkey holds a dented silver baby cup. After a few songs the monkey visits tables to beg for coins by presenting the baby cup.

Sidewalk serenades are an important part of the French ambiance. I walk slowly as I pass the cafes to reach the river only two hundred steps away. I listen to hear the classic songs about romance in Paris made famous by Edith Piaf, Maurice Chevalier and others.

The large floating tourist boat of the Bateaux-Mouches fleet is docked in front of Pont d'Alma, the bridge crossing the Seine near the Cathedral. It travels back and forth on the Seine for about an hour while a loudspeaker explains to the tourists the scenes they are observing. About two hundred people can sit on wooden chairs placed in horizontal rows on an open top deck. The Bateaux-Mouches is ugly. It seeks to look nice but fails. The red plastic geraniums in their plastic pots don't help the cause. This vessel was not built to be beautiful but to carry as many people as possible. It is a ferry without cars. It brings to mind a London tour bus with an upper deck filled with people being told what they are seeing. On the Seine they are told what they are seeing in French and English. Added translations such as Arabic, Japanese, Chinese and other major languages are available in handouts at the gangplank. This is a floating Tower of Babel. Paris is a mistress who seduces tourists from around the world to experience her charms and pay for her delights. She is not selective whom she seduces. New customers appear every weekend, especially in summer months. The madam wants money and lovers pay. The Bateaux is a favorite attraction.

To avoid the activity on the deck above me I move aft, and through a closed door I enter a small open place on the main deck. There are three or four empty chairs and a view of the left and right banks from nearer the water level. There is another loudspeaker in the ceiling of my hidden kingdom. The views are better on the top deck. When the weather is good the sightseers prefer to be up there. In poor weather they move downstairs to a large protected deck with similar seating arrangements. My private sanctuary remains unknown. Years ago I discovered that I could stand on a chair, disconnect the wire leading to a small speaker in the ceiling, and replace it at the end of the hour. I didn't want to listen to the chatter from above. In my memories of these times, I usually have a ham and cheese baguette with a coke. During our eleven years in Paris I spent numerous lunch hours through wind, rain, and sun on this barge. Water of any kind, from an ocean to a parking lot puddle, provides catharsis for me. The Bateaux-Mouches has been my getaway—my escape from the joys, blessings, and disappointments of being a priest. My memories are the life blood of my soul. They make up who I am and who I have become. Their drama is always with me.

A young mother is informed that there is a lump in her breast. A student spending a junior year abroad receives a "Dear John" letter from the girl in the States whom he had hoped to marry. I must deal with a layman in the cathedral who is a bully. Memories come to me of praying at a death bed in a hospital and holding the hand of one who fears the next few minutes. I recall the joy of being in the same hospital at a different bed on a different floor a few hours later holding hands with new parents and giving thanks to God for a healthy baby boy born forty five minutes earlier. A father of two teenagers wants to see me. He is burdened with guilt and shame over an adulterous mistake. He mostly fears being discovered.

A European gentleman has been attending noon time services. He is tastefully dressed as a Parisian but his words indicate an Argentine diplomat. Later in the day he asks to talk me. He sounds anxious.

We sit alone in silence in a side chapel. No tourists visit at that hour. He breaks the silence by talking about his life and his youth, growing up in Argentina. After pauses and silences he explains why he needs to talk to someone. He asks me if God would forgive him for a sin he had committed. I assure him that God's business is to forgive and that our God is a loving God. That is all I say. I listen and don't ask questions. There is silence.

His head is bowed. Hands grip his knees. Words sound forced as he speaks. In a soft whisper with eyes closed, he admits to being the arms dealer who sold an Exocet missile to the Argentine Air Force. This missile subsequently disabled and sunk the British missile destroyer HMS Sheffield on May 4, 1982 in the battle of the Falklands. The ship sank after being consumed by flames and engulfed in high seas. Twenty English sailors lost their lives. As he speaks, that act of war is front page news in the world wide press and breaking news on television.

The Cathedral is now alive. It breathes in silence. Mighty stone walls that keep out summer heat and winds of winter are now shielding two immovable souls huddled together in a small side chapel. It is rush hour in Paris but the rude sounds of motor bikes, trucks, and taxis outside on the Avenue George V cannot invade this 'mighty fortress of our God.' Now a stronger phenomenon occurs as if to demonstrate God's mighty power.

All at once, swiftly moving puffs of white clouds are rushing across the face of the sun. This celestial dance miles above the earth is reaching down and touching the ancient stained glass windows high in the walls of the transept, creating new visions and painting pictures inside the Cathedral.

Streams of red and blue and green dots and lines scoot across pews, stalls, lecterns, pulpits and pillars to make a pilgrimage to the main altar and offer their abstract tracings to their maker. The nave is filled with quick movements, colored movements, and pencil thin lines which form rows up one aisle and down another. Technicolor dots elongate for an instant then disappear. They meld one with another in indescribable beauty. Crisscrossing the center aisle they find momentary rest in a pew, then blend in the next pew to make more colors and restart a new journey around the cathedral. Then, the remaining lights fade as the few wisps of clouds disappear.

We are astounded, humbled, and stunned. An exhibit of color, majesty and silence has taken place. I have never in my life seen nor ever expect to see again such a dramatic show. Our mouths are wide open in awe at what we have experienced, knowing that no liturgies, hymns, prayers, sermons, weddings, or funerals can compete with what we have just seen, together, for only this minute. This must have been the feeling of the centurion at the foot of the Cross when, as Christ utters the words. "Into Thy hands I commend my spirit", a lightning flash, for just a second, opened up the landscape as far as the eye could see. The two of us stand. My unknown companion looks me in the eye. He whispers, "Thank you for listening and for your words of strength," shakes my hand and departs.

I watch him walk away. I had spoken only a short sentence. I did not pray with him. I missed a chance to tell him the good news that a sinner who asks for forgiveness can be open to God's grace. I never saw the man again. In my life since, I have wished I could relive those moments in order to offer a small gesture, or quiet words that might have been meaningful to him. As years have gone by, I have sometimes thought of this nameless and suffering man. I somehow hope that those quiet moments and the beauty of the cathedral on that late afternoon spoke to him as well. Perhaps through the wonders of the sun and clouds and ancient stained glass, God somehow reached this man's tortured soul.

My life as a priest is one of constant change, of shame and happiness, of success and failure, truth and lies. Life is beautiful and tragic. Evidence of this is always present in a congregation as it is within my own heart and soul.

It is ironic that some sought refuge on their lunch hour at the Cathedral to seek the same blessings of peace and quiet that I seek when I go to the Bateaux-Mouches. It was important to spend part of my day alone, away from others, and from the Cathedral. The boat had become my chapel. It provided a good time to pray, give thanks, and ask forgiveness.

I think back to one occasion on which I am sitting alone in my floating "chapel" when the door opens from the main deck. An oddly dressed, elderly woman in a multi-colored short sleeved dress and wide brimmed black hat enters. Wispy black hair extends from beneath the hat and her face appears never to have laughed or even to have smiled. I do not find her interesting. She sits near me to stare into space without saying hello or recognizing my presence. Why did this happen today? I give up trying to be alone with my thoughts. I feel this lunch hour to be a waste of time. Out of the corner of my eye I watch her. Bent over, she holds her head in her hands and stares into space.

On the inside of her arm are tattooed a series of numbers, and when I notice the tattoo, I am stunned. It is often said that God works in strange ways. This unattractive person who is an intruder becomes a heroine in my eyes. She is a Jewish survivor of a Nazi death camp. I want to say something but do not know what to say or how to say it. I am in the presence of a person of great significance. I had heard about such people but never before identified one. When the hour is over I stand and hold the door open for this woman. As she approaches, I say, 'Shalom aleichem, Madame'. Peace be to you. That night I think about this Jewish woman. I had said only three words to her but she, in fact, opened a door in my life. It was she who provided a moment of grace in my evening devotions that night.

St. Paul says in his letter to the Hebrews: 'Do not neglect to show hospitality to strangers, for by doing so some have entertained angels. Remember those who are being tortured as though you yourselves were being tortured.' I have experienced firsthand the need for this admonition, and it has left me changed.

I did accept the call to be the rector of Christ Church in Cincinnati, Ohio. As I approached the end of my stay in Paris and my service to the American Cathedral, I was unsure as to whether I felt happy or sad. When I ended my final hour on the Bateaux, I did not experience my usual sense of peace. In two days, I would announce at the Sunday service that I would be leaving Paris to become the rector of Christ Church in Cincinnati Ohio.

I would leave Paris in six weeks. I was excited about the future but how I would miss France!

CHAPTER TEN

CHRIST CHURCH, CINCINNATI

The city of Cincinnati was in trouble. It was a time of exploding racial tensions. The black community was angry and blamed the white establishment for the troubles. Christ Church and other parishes in the city were trying to calm the situation and bring peace to the city. At this same time Christ Church was searching for a rector. The newly elected Bishop in the Diocese of Southern Ohio, The Right Reverend Herbert Thompson, thought that because I had marched with Martin Luther King in Alabama it would mean something positive to the black activists if I would be their rector.

I had met Herb Thompson at the General Theological Seminary in New York City in the 'sixties where we were students together. Herb was a charismatic leader and a man of strong faith. We liked each other but went our separate ways after graduation. Twenty years later, the vacancy at Christ Church had come to his attention. He assured the congregation of his help in their search and reminded them that he must give final approval for the person they wished to hire. He had then called me in Paris to discuss the vacancy at Christ Church. I tried to persuade him that his plan would not work.

"Just because I believe in the just causes of unrest in our country over racial divides, and participated in a march for freedom years ago, does not make me able to solve the problems in Cincinnati," I argued. "You are an African American Bishop. Look for a black priest like yourself to come to the Christ Church."

He did not feel the congregation was ready to accept a black priest, or even a woman, to be its leader. He said that someday that would happen; that the present might be the time for a black priest to be on the staff, but not as rector. He asked me to reconsider.

I knew my life would change in so many ways if I accepted a call. I didn't sleep well for the next few days. On a stormy Friday night at 2:30 a.m., I had leaned over in bed and whispered to Patsy,

"I can't sleep. Are you awake?"

"Yes, I am wide awake and I guess you are going to Cincinnati if you get a call. If you go, don't worry about me. I'll call you every weekend from Paris!"

"You can't be serious?"

"No, of course not. Whither thou goest, I go."

Thus, we arrived late on a steamy August afternoon in Cincinnati. It had not rained for days. The city was melting. We stayed the night at the Queen City Club adjacent to Christ Church and the baseball stadium. The trip from Paris had been tiring. We fell asleep early because of jet lag. An hour later we were awake, confused and scared. The sounds of gunshots and bombs reverberated in our room. The committee had been right when they talked about riots.

Security had been at a high pitch when we had left Paris. Terrorist attacks threatened American and Jewish establishments. The Paris cathedral had increased security precautions. We were worried now about a bomb attack in Cincinnati. I called the front desk to ask if the Club were being attacked.

"No, sir," the answer came. "Those firecrackers and rockets are from the stadium. Someone has hit a home run for the Reds!"

*   *   *

When I first saw Christ Church, I was shocked. It looked like a Caribbean airport gone bankrupt. The next afternoon I sat with the vestry and listened to a back and forth discussion among the members about problems and hopes for the parish. There was no mention of God or Jesus. They seemed lost in the overwhelming fumes of talk about cash. The discussion was about endowments. This was one of the richest parishes in the Episcopal Church with endowments of almost one hundred million dollars!

I was uneasy. I wanted to discuss the faith. They wanted to discuss money. They wanted me to protect their money. I wanted to protect their faith. That was my job. I began to think that the church fathers should have called the CEO of J.P. Morgan Bank & Trust Company to be their priest.

Had I made a mistake? Had they made a mistake? I did not want them to sense my trepidation. I nodded my head as if everything were alright. I held back and said nothing. This was not the time to show my apprehension. St. Paul said, "Speak the truth in love." I wanted and needed to love these people before I expressed anxieties and doubts about their secular icons.

*   *   *

These were sad times at Christ Church. Clergy in the parish had been forced to leave. There had been a drop in membership and a rise of distrust in the pews. Shortly after I arrived the assistant had resigned. I was alone, terribly alone, in a foreign country. I felt like the monkey in the zoo. Everyone knows the monkey but the monkey just sees faces.

One Sunday morning soon after my arrival, our Bishop came to lead the service for the Institution of a new Rector. I welcomed Bishop Thompson to the congregation and briefly spoke about the role of a Bishop in the Episcopal Church.

I explained that we believe that the Bishop is the head of the Diocese, including the parishes. I was now officially the Rector of Christ Church. The Bishop was my leader. The 'cathedra' or Bishop's chair is in the altar area of every church in the Diocese. It is a reminder to laity and clergy that Bishops are important. They confirm members, ordain priests and deacons, institute rectors, settle disputes and grant permission to hold back or marry divorced members. It has been said "where the Bishop is, there the church is".

This frank statement surprised some of our people who never thought a Bishop had such power. They thought the parish was meant to be owned and operated by the elected leadership on the vestry.

It is said that the longest distance to the Bishop's office was from Christ Church, even though it is obvious we were neighbors on Fourth and Sycamore. I planned to change this feeling in my announcements and words of welcome. Bishop Thompson and I were standing together on the steps to the altar. I turned to face him, took his hand, and said, "Bishop, in the name of Jesus Christ our Lord and Savior, I greet you on behalf of your people in Christ Church. I am a Bishop's man. I shall be your hands in this parish. Use me as you will. When you need me I shall be here for you."

We were beginning to create a new atmosphere that would lead us in new directions for new seasons. We had a few minutes alone after the service. He gave me a hug and said, "Thank you, James, my friend. I loved every word you said. You made me feel like a Bishop for this place." It marked a new beginning of a spiritual and lifelong friendship. Our mutual loneliness and the realization that we needed each other was a blessing for both of us.

*   *   *

I had been in the parish for only two weeks when people started asking if I had met Rawson. Who is this man? I was looking forward to meeting him.

My curiosity was answered by my warden.

"His name is J. Rawson Collins. People know him as Rawson. He is a giant in the parish, in the Diocese, and in the city and is admired by many. He knows the history of Christ Church. He understands the numerous accounts in the endowment—the restrictions, the amounts, and its history, including the Dean's Discretionary Fund that has millions and remains the most controversial account because it is at the sole discretion of the Dean.

"Rawson has been a member of every committee in Christ Church, with the exception of the Episcopal Church Women. I am sure he will call on you. He loves this place."

I wondered why, when discussing Christ Church, people in both the parish and the diocese always began with the size of the endowment and the turnover in parish priests. Could Rawson explain this to me? Was it admiration or jealousy that made me want to meet him? Taking the initiative, I invited him to lunch the next day.

A one-hour lunch lasted for three and a half hours. I was enthralled. I understood why folks talked about him as though he were a living legend. Rawson was in his eighties and lived alone, having never married. I was told he was wealthy, yet his suit and shirt were wrinkled. An outrageously messy Stetson hat made me imagine he had slept in it. The sole of his left shoe had a hole. When he spoke, however, his words and his insight gave credence to the perception that Rawson was smart and sophisticated. Rawson spoke in an untroubled tone that made people stop talking and listen to what he was saying. No one minded his appearance. Cincinnati's finest widows tried to capture his attention but, to their sorrow, it was no use.

The grace and the sins of Christ church were deliberated over grilled cheese sandwiches, chips and iced tea. I listened to him march through the nineteenth and twentieth century history of Cincinnati and Christ Church. The sins of pride and racism had raised their heads in each generation but at the same time, the great gift of grace through outreach had set examples for urban churches throughout our country, especially in New York City and Boston. Some believed then and still do today, that we are a club of right minded neighbors. We love our liturgy and our propriety. Anglican history and our prayer book seem to bestow on us a special blessing. Some think we were baptized into that propriety. We love our church but know that we must begin thinking that when the 11:00 o'clock Sunday service ends at noon, true service begins. Our forefathers believed in that kind of Christian action.

In earlier years there was a large, low rent community of city workers within a few blocks of the Parish known as the Basin Area. Early records, reports and minutes of Parish societies show their work in the Basin Area in the 1850's, 1860's, and 1870's. These reports are in the library of the Cincinnati Historical Society. There are records from the Chancel Guild, the Girls' Friendly Society, the Gleaners, and the Women's Auxiliary. The Men's Club of the Parish House kept their own yearbooks for years. Scrapbooks of newspaper clippings speak of great athletic teams in the early 1900's in the Parish gymnasium and the summer camp owned by the Parish. The outreach activities in these early years were focused on the Basin Area. When that area became gentrified, outreach programs were undermined.

During those early years there was a line drawn in the sand. This line was drawn not only in the Southern states but throughout the country. There were black churches. There were white churches. There was white music. There was black music. There was propriety in white liturgy. There was spontaneity in black liturgy.

Human relations in our broken city needed prominent and immediate attention. Evangelism and outreach would have to be practiced as well as preached. Check-passing programs would not be enough. This major league effort would have to be innovative and large in scale. All of this was the subject of our conversation on that day.

Rawson and I had other lunches together and decided to meet every two weeks. The church was furthermore blessed with two wise wardens who met regularly with me to discuss our opportunities and problems. In the first year I listened to guilds and groups of young married couples, teenagers, and shut-ins that came together to talk about our church and how could we do a better job in ministry, education, fellowship, and stewardship.

*   *   *

The fall season passed unnoticed. I was putting energy, hopes, prayers, and my life into Christ Church. I existed only for that place. My family, friends, and the rest of the world with its charms and delights became secondary. I was working seven days a week. I had a passion to know this congregation and the city.

It was becoming clear to me that the hundred million dollar endowment was embalming fluid. It was killing our giving spirit and turning our Church into a club. It seemed that everybody had secrets. The vestry room reminded me of an armed bunker in a far off corner of the Church, wrapped in Byzantine secrecy. It was a forbidding room resembling a cellblock. Parishioners were not asked to attend meetings. I tried to encourage parishioners' attendance at meetings so that they could become more aware of our blessings and our challenges as a church. Visitors were given voice but no vote. Transparency would have to be established both in finances and in committee processes.

I conveyed my feelings on the endowment. It had become a problem because it was affecting personal giving and outreach programs. The issue raised its head in the annual stewardship campaign. I was surprised and saddened when I saw the campaign results. It was a somber moment when the pledged amount was published. Few cared. The response was, "we have the endowment." Pledging five dollars a week indicates little or no interest in missionary outreach, and Sunday attendance is poor. Increase that same five dollar pledge to one hundred dollars a week and interest in programs and church attendance become part of one's life. Pledging is a barometer for measuring the health of a parish.

Many members had little sympathy for government welfare so I pointed out that Christ Church was a welfare parish. Somebody else was paying our way. Generous trust funds in the name of the parish created by forefathers kept alive a way of life for our members. We were sustained by welfare. Much of the endowment came from William C. Procter, a founder of Procter and Gamble.

The committees that dealt with financial matters were lifelong members and leaders in Cincinnati business firms. Funds were controlled by four or five wealthy men in the congregation. The vestry had confidence in these stalwart members. Outside professional help was not considered necessary. With vacancies occurring because of deaths, this small group agreed to use outside firms. During this time we were able to replace members of other committees due to death or resignations. New members encouraged recommendations to spend more of the interest return in Christian outreach in our city. We had some outreach projects but not yet enough parishioner involvement.

We sought to double our congregation and eventually began to pick up speed. A new family joined us from another Episcopal church. The family had asked to be transferred. I did not want clergy accusing me of sheep stealing. The priest from the nearby parish called me to say thank you and good luck. After one month I knew why he had thanked me!

One Sunday a family of four attended for the first time. When I greeted them at the front door after the service, the wife loudly proclaimed that they were shopping for a parish church. They wanted a good Sunday school, good music, thoughtful sermons and active programs. I replied that we were shopping for parishioners. We needed members who would attend on Sundays, pledge to support the Church, become involved in our programs and learn more about Jesus.

I neglected to tell the whole truth. The Sunday school was baby sitting hour for children. Our total Sunday school enrollment was about fifteen on a good Sunday. Its saving grace was the loyalty of a few committed teachers. The teenage program had a few members. Half of them would only show up on the Sunday when they were acolytes. I didn't have an active program for adults. If I were that woman who was searching, I would not have returned the next Sunday.

In every parish there are wolves in the basement "roaring around seeking whom they can devour." There are members who watch carefully how the new rector will handle this problem of those wolves bred by previous rectors. It was now my time to step up and begin making changes in entrenched mind sets. Change is usually painful. This was not going to be easy. My honeymoon was coming to an end but now there would also be help from supporters within.

*   *   *

Time passed quickly. Some goals and plans never developed the way I had hoped. Families moved to suburbs for better schools. Older members who had been leaders now worshipped God on that other shore. I had been at Christ Church for some years. The church was worn out and unsightly. There was no handicap access in the church or adjacent classrooms and offices. The heating and air-conditioning system was an antique and expensive to operate. We had so many systems to repair and replace. I formed a vision of renovating our worn down and outdated buildings and ultimately making Christ Church into a Cathedral.

A special meeting was called to meet with the Bishop to listen to his own dream for a central place to worship and to have large celebrations. He talked about a place for confirmations, ordinations, and noted speakers. The diocesan office building was suitable for administration but not for other purposes. The Bishop spoke of a spiritual center for our churches, an ecumenical place where men and women of different faiths could gather. Christ Church was large enough and well-placed in the center of the city. The Bishop was at his best. It was an inspired meeting. A vote was taken to proceed. The result was almost unanimous. Both Herb and I were delighted. But there were two abstentions. I knew in advance that these two older members would not want to change. "Why change now?" they reasoned.

I was being blamed for this plan by those in the pews who were uneasy so I decided to let my clergy staff and some vestry people speak for me. Initial cost projections were initially set at two million dollars and this figure was announced to the congregation. I knew differently. I thought it might be eight million. I kept my mouth shut. It finally ended up costing nine million. This was not going to be easy. It would mean using the endowment. The sacred icon.

I perceived now a racist element to the club mentality, winding its poisonous tendrils into our church. Two couples who had recently become members wanted to pull up the bridge and stop pushing for those new members whom they knew would join if the church were to be enlarged. Many members who had spent their lives in the parish didn't want change in our social makeup. Their reaction surprised me. I was afraid that they would not accept what I had started. Our city, its churches, its clubs, its history have been plagued by this sin of racism. We could not seem to escape its hideous history in our lives.

The next step, in which the fighting, the fears and the possible defeat of the Cathedral plan would occur, had arrived. There was to be no turning back. Difficulties were obvious. The entrenched old timers who did not see a need for change kept up a tiresome cacophony. This church structure and its status as a parish had been unchanged since 1817 and that history since 1817 was their pride. The building would have a new look and cost millions of dollars. The name would change from Church to Cathedral. We would become a spiritual home for the Bishop and have a significant ministry to and with the churches in the Diocese. We would be making significant withdrawals from the endowment. Before I jumped in with my enthusiasm there should be some age and longevity endorsing this plan. I was still considered a newcomer even though I had been in this position for several years now.

An architect was hired and we were able to hear his ideas and see drawings. When the old group saw the sketches, they saw their shadow and retreated into their burrows. To spend a lot of money to change the life of Christ Church amounted to heresy and I was becoming the chief priest of the heretics.

The Bishop remained a strong voice. Together we formed a team. Our friendship formed so many years before was a treasure. He had initiated the idea of Christ Church becoming a cathedral. It made sense. The Diocese needed a cathedral. Christ Church was the only choice.

Rawson supported this proposal as well. He patiently explained to the skeptical how much money could be saved with new electrical, heating, and cooling systems. The new structure would be handicapped accessible. Modern kitchen equipment could serve meals for large meeting or gatherings. Elevators would be installed to bring people to different floors. Clergy offices would be renewed. The Internet would be available with new wiring. Our present system was ancient, troublesome and expensive.

Rawson paid to have a wooden model created by the architect and this was placed in full view of everyone entering the church. We started getting good press. Excitement was born.

I had been convinced that this job was too big for me and that the congregation was hung up on its own egos. I had been ready to quit. But Rawson and Herb Thompson, the Bishop, understood my fears and disillusionment and kept me in one piece. They agreed that the church needed a new look, not only in its physical appearance, but in the spiritual life of the congregation. With their strong leadership, the dream of a Cathedral now stood a chance.

Now I asked for God's angels to come and anoint the idea. Another meeting with the Bishop was scheduled at which time we would vote on the new constitution and this plan would either fall apart or come together.

*   *   *

The present vestry and a few outsiders gathered in the sanctuary on a sunny afternoon in the spring. This sanctuary was a place where prayerful decisions had been decided throughout time. Year after year, week after week this space had attracted sinners and saints. It was holy ground.

Voices were subdued. Arguments, hopes, and ideas were presented with gracious words and kind intentions. This was Herbert Thompson's milieu. He was the one who could gently quiet the troubled waters of contentious affairs. I had been in places where tension and animosity were winning the hour. People would stop arguing when he appeared, and in moments, he would have men and women hanging on his words. He was able to talk about God and bring a Holy Spirit into the midst. He was a healer of wounded spirits.

On that day, I met him outside the chapel and said, "Herb, this is where the war begins. Do your thing."

"James, you are wrong," he replied. "This is where God's grace wins the peace."

We entered the chapel. The Bishop sat on his sedilia and faced the vestry. You could hear the silence. He bowed his head and remained still. We waited, we watched, we listened. The silence was playing havoc with my nerves. Why didn't he speak? We weren't here to sit in silence.

Finally, he spoke. God bless Christ Church, its parishioners, its vestry and clergy. We listened. He softly recited the gracious history of our parish's best moments—the many times since the 1800's when we faced challenges in the Basin Area, and our generous contributions to the Diocese and the National Church. He thanked God for so many years of service. He mentioned the Taft family who gave our country a president and the many young men who had given their lives in our country's service. Legions grew up in this place and contributed to worthy causes in our city and beyond, and now these saints worshipped God on that other shore.

He talked about that moment and why he was there on that day. Our diocese needed a space for large services. It needed a place where visiting Bishops, ecumenical visitors and programs could be presented. The city needed a Cathedral.

When he finished this short history there were not many dry eyes and there was a change in the chapel. There was an aura of holiness. He stood up and said, "The church is calling on you again. We need you." He knew when to stop. He blessed us, thanked us for listening, and left.

A motion was made to form a joint committee from the Diocese and Christ Church that would create a new constitution for a cathedral. This was a step in the right direction. New ministries were in the future for the Diocese and the city, which would lift us out of the abyss of mediocrity. That was an exciting moment.

I knew that day was a beginning. The euphoria would wear off and details in the rebuilding efforts would present problems but we had a new vision. Alleluia!

The next time that Patsy and I attended a Reds game at the stadium, the rockets and firecrackers went off for a home run once again, but this time I felt that it was a message from God to never give up hope.

Today the congregation has a small number of African Americans in its membership. There is hope for a wider representation as the church reaches out to the African American neighborhoods. The outreach budget for Christ Church Cathedral was a quarter of a million dollars during my final year. The church's adults teach and work in city schools. Evangelism and outreach will continue if the Cathedral is to follow its historic work in the city and beyond. We have a God given gift to give, which will inspire our generation and generations to come.

CHAPTER ELEVEN

WE BATTLE CANCER

My doctor calls at three o' clock in the afternoon. He wants to speak with me immediately. An MRI has indicated that I have an esophageal tumor symptomatic of cancer. I am scared. Patsy is in Europe guiding a group of museum art directors in France. She will not return until tomorrow night. I can't sleep this night. I want to talk to someone but will have to wait a day until I see my wife. My life is coming to an end.

I pick Patsy up at the airport in the evening. She gets into the car and I cry. I'm embarrassed. She's alarmed. I explain what happened at the doctor's office. She is calm. I'm a mess. In silence, we head to a restaurant for a meal. I don't want to go home.

Patsy invades the silence:

"From this moment on we are preparing for war. Together we are going to beat cancer."

I am in agreement but say nothing. When one person in a family gets cancer the whole family suffers. I wonder how one prepares for war against cancer.

My last thoughts before falling asleep this night are to ask God for help and strength. There will be other helpers but God is my first line of defense. Family and friends who are joining in prayer to get me through this battle have volunteered for the fight with their love and concern. When one gets cancer, tell friends. They want to help.

The rest of the week is devoted to meeting an oncologist, radiologist, and surgeon. They agree that my case needs aggressive therapy. This information doesn't mean much to me at this time. I will understand the meaning of this later.

The next day at the doctor's office, a small plastic patch the size of a quarter is inserted under my skin as a weapon against this monster, cancer. The patch placed in my chest receives chemo and other medications. I am to carry a bag filled with chemo around my waist. This bag is attached to a transistor-like apparatus worn on my belt or carried in my hand. A plastic cord within a small tube, leads from the transistor to the patch. This battery operated black box will relay chemo into my body day and night without a break.

Patsy and I are in bed for the night. Lights are out. Nothing moves. We are awake, stony still, and holding hands under the sheets. The only sounds are sounds of silence. Then it comes and hits us in the face! It's only a tiny whisper. Swish, that's it—just a tiny swish. It's over in a second only to make another appearance in two minutes. This is the sound of the chemo being sent to find its way through the tubes into my body. I imagine a Zamboni sliding up and down and back and forth scraping away intruders and at the same time undermining my system. Chemo is breaking down the cancer but doing damage to other organs that I hope will return to their original structure. The cancerous tissue will dissolve. There is a war going on inside of me. Am I to be a winner or a loser? I have no appetite, no energy, no interest in conversation, television, or reading. Life is a struggle. My mouth is full of sores. Which is worse, chemo or cancer? I am dying. So what!

The chemo is composed primarily of a chemical called 5-FU. It didn't take us long to give 5-FU a nickname which I shall leave to your imagination. I now understand what the doctors meant by aggressive therapy.

To this day, ten years later, I remember the swishes.

In six weeks, chemo and radiation are finished. I am a zombie. I don't care what happens. I fall asleep in strange places, like on a park bench or an empty chair in Macy's. Sometimes my wife can't find me. Store clerks have to wake me up. I'm sure people walking in the park think I'm homeless. Maybe I am. Hopeless and homeless—that's me. Tomorrow the surgeon has his turn. I hope he has a good night's sleep! Is all this worth it?

I wake up in the intensive care ward. Six IVs are scattered over my worn body planted in every orifice I own. Stitches cover my chest and back. They aren't plain old stitches. They are huge aluminum staples. I decide to ask for anesthesia or a suicide pill before they are removed. This will hurt. My stomach has been displaced. It is cut in half and moved up closer to my chin. How am I supposed to survive? Yet, it is the removal of the stitches that terrifies me the most. You win, God. I give up!

The morning of the third day is my D-day. Charles, the ward's head nurse who has been taking care of me approaches my bed. Charles is a monster. He must be a linebacker for the Cincinnati Bengals on his day off. He is as tall as the IV stand next to me and probably weighs a ton. He is carrying an ugly steel instrument which resembles a staple remover and that's what it is.

"Please Charles don't do this to me," I beg.

"You won't even feel it."

"I'll bet you tell everyone that, and it's going to kill me."

"Preacher! Don't be a cupcake. Be a man!"

"I give up. Rip the bastards out and kill me."

Charles is right. Looks are misleading. I don't feel a thing.

Charles comes to me as I am rolled out of the IC ward to a room downstairs.

"Don't worry cupcake, you're a good man and will make it. Come back and see me sometime."

I can't talk. I am choked up. This gentle grizzly took care of me. I am touched by his ministry of healing.

The hospital keeps me for five more days and starts me on Jello. After almost a week, the head nurse informs me that I can go home once I have a bowel movement.

"You must be crazy," I say. "I haven't eaten for almost a week. Nothing will work."

"Then we shall have to put something in your rectum to make it work."

"Oh, no, you won't. I never want another IV, needle or catheter and surely not some machine or gadget put up my butt!'

'Well then, you will have to stay here. Think about it.'

I am up against Nurse Cratchit. She is going to win. I want to go home. In my lifetime I have prayed for weird things, but never to produce evidence for a bed pan.

Two hours later God answers my prayer. I can go home.

I am now in the care of my wife who has healing hands and a God given patience. The heavy armament is now on my side, accompanied by immediate family and the prayers of friends. There are prayers from parishioners in other parishes. Prayers from friends in Europe, from Roman Catholic friends, from Jewish friends. There are the thoughts of my friends who are non-believers. There is an avalanche of cards and letters. My daughter-in-law has written to President George Bush telling him of my plight and of my fondness for him when he visited the Cathedral in Paris, and now the President sends a letter from the White House! Bishop Thompson visits every day when we share Morning or Evening Prayer.

One day, the Bishop comes in the morning and appears again in the evening. This scares me.

"You were here once today. Why did you come again? Do you know something I don't know? Give me the bad news."

"No, I was having a bad day and I wanted to pray with you."

Wow! What a man. Why can't I be more like him? My Bishop is a saint who is so transparent, so honest. He is a man of God. I love him.

I am beginning to feel guilty with all this attention from so many. What if I die? Would that outcome affect their belief in God? I want to get better for their sakes. This sounds strange but sometimes I think in strange ways.

I stay in the apartment for a week. Our front balcony is on the second floor overlooking a park across Fourth Street. I sit in my lawn chair and watch activities of early commuter traffic. It is June in the park. I have a miraculous sense of spring and feel inspired by the sight of clouds meandering across the sky and of the pear trees and dogwoods standing tall in measured rows. I breathe in the fragrance of tulips and daffodils, lilies of the valley, and the scent of newly cut grass. Cars pass by on Fourth Street, occasionally sounding a horn. A broken down Ford convertible filled with four African American teenagers has a boom box sounding at a deafening volume. I feel a need to get out of this apartment and sit on the bench across the street but I am unsteady on my feet. Patsy does not want to help me get across the street because she might not be able to pick me up if I stumble. There is another problem. I don't have any pants or belts to use. I have lost over forty pounds and my pants could fit an elephant. I am a string bean. I have been in slippers and bathrobe since I have been home and now I need a closet full of new clothes. I weave a clothes line through the belt loops to hold up bunched pants. But there is no time to waste. Here is my chance. Pasty is in town and will be gone for another two hours.

I leave the apartment in my bathrobe and slippers, take the elevator to the lobby and leave the building. When I reach the park bench after carefully crossing the street, I feel like a million dollars. Three minutes ago I was locked up in my home. Now a free man, I wonder if any before me have ever made such a brave journey in dangerous territory clad only in bathrobe and slippers?

* * *

Our son Jason is the rector of a small parish in Columbus, Ohio, a two-hour drive from Cincinnati. He volunteers to come down early in the mornings to stay with me in the park for a couple of hours each week, and to walk me back and forth across hectic Fourth Street during the morning rush hour. He has a busy job. I am getting stronger so I won't need him after another week. Once I am in the park I can walk on the paths with my cane and put strength back in my legs. I never mention to anyone that I have already made the maiden voyage.

One morning Jason is helping me cross the street. We sit on the bench together. I need a short rest.

"Dad, how are you feeling today?" he asks.

"Jace, I get cramps and have cystitis."

"Dad, you are a girl. Girls get cramps and cystitis. What are my friends going to think when they discover my Dad is a girl?

"By the way, I am arranging an appointment for you with a world famous doctor."

"I don't need another doctor," I say. "I have three great men who take care of me. Who is this 'world class' healer that you want me to see?"

"Dr. Kevorkian!

"Dad, just in case you decide to want to 'check-out' in the next few days, would you mind talking to me about the will. I hope you realize I love you more than my brother Jon. He doesn't commute to see you two or three times a week, even though he lives in California!"

Jason has me laughing so hard I am crying. His humor keeps his mother and me both laughing—something our home needs so much at this time.

The days go by and I begin to heal. I want to believe my friends when they tell me I look better. They are probably stuck for something to say. I order some new clothes and get rid of the clothesline. I am able to walk two blocks to the office and sit in my office and stare out the window.

I take a Sunday service with no evident problems except exhaustion. Standing for long periods is strenuous. When greeting parishioners after the service, I brace myself half sitting and half standing on a high stool.

Clearly, I am lacking in energy, that one resource so necessary to the priesthood whether one serves in the smallest mission in our worldwide church or the largest cathedral on earth.

I bear in mind that I am approaching retirement age and that our work on the renovation of the Christ Church Cathedral in Cincinnati is finally approaching an end. I decide that this evening I shall discuss with my family the idea of retiring.

CHAPTER TWELVE

RAWSON'S DEATH

I answer the phone. I have been expecting this call.

"Rawson is dying. Come immediately."

I am home resting. It is late in the afternoon. I have been regaining strength but this is taking more time than expected. I have been home from the hospital for almost three weeks. After five minutes I am able to walk slowly with a vague shuffle. I need to get to my friend's bedside.

For me, dressing has become an excuse to sit down. Each possible article of clothing is put on from a seated position. I only stand to pull up my pants. I am going to need every ounce of strength for the hour ahead.

I take a portable communion set once owned by Paul Moore, the great Bishop of New York, and given to me by a dear friend. I tell Patsy I am ready to leave. She offers to drive me to Rawson's apartment. We stop at the front door of the apartment building so that I don't have to walk from the parking area.

Going through the lobby I make it to the elevator. Thank God it opens so I don't have to wait. In the elevator there is a small seat in the corner. I sit whenever I see a seat. Walking down a long hall, I reach my friend's spacious apartment as I am beginning to tire. I pray God will give me strength to do my job as a priest.

Betty, the maid, answers the door. She has been with Rawson for years. She is stunned by my appearance and wants to talk. I explain that I am tired. I must see Rawson now.

If my appearance frightens Betty it doesn't bother Rawson. The first thing he says is, "How is your health? It seems everyone in Cincinnati knows about your cancer and is praying for you. Especially the members in this household."

"I guess I'm doing all right. How about you?"

"I'm not going to make it, Jim."

His voice is weak. He is on his back looking uncomfortable. Numerous flower vases placed on tables, window sills, and ledges are overkill in this room. It resembles an undertaker's parlor. I slowly lift his head and shoulders and carefully place two pillows behind him.

It is warm in the room. His feet are sticking out under the top sheet. This bothers me because he only has one sock on. Where is the other one? A urinal stands guard on a bedside table.

I watch him for a minute. He seems to be asleep. I have my communion set with me and begin the brief home service. A psalm, a shortened New Testament lesson, ancient prayers and some wine and bread consecrated from last Sunday's Service.

I always stand at a communion service whether in church, hospital or home. Not today. We are alone. I have to use a chair.

"Can you hear me, Rawson?"

With his eyes still closed and in a weak slow voice he whispers, "What are you waiting for Jim? Let's go."

I begin the short service. After the service I shall want to stay with him for a time and know I must rest for a minute.

"Rawson, you are loved by many including me."

I bow my head, and begin the Twenty-third Psalm. These beloved Hebrew verses have been a comfort to generations of people who need strength and courage in dark hours. The only other sound in this room is Rawson's erratic breathing. For a few moments this space with its death bed, has become a shrine, a holy place. Sheets and blankets are palls for a worn out body.

"Lord now lettest thou thy servant depart in peace according to thy word. For mine eyes have seen thy salvation which thou hast prepared before the face of all people. To be a light to lighten the Gentiles and to be the Glory of thy people Israel."

I have the feeling his soul is no longer with me. Has my friend left these earthly bounds to awake in a new and finer place? I see no movement.

I believe God appears as a gentle friend and loving father in those last minutes of our lives. The gracious Lord took my friend by the hand as they went together on his last journey. Final minutes are serene and peaceful for many of the children of God. How do I know this? I don't know. Often there is a quiet peace in one's face when death stands nearby.

"May the God of peace, who brought again from the dead our Lord Jesus, the great shepherd of the sheep, by the blood of the eternal covenant, equip you with everything good that you may do his will, working in you that which is pleasing in his sight."

What happens next is something I shall carry with me to the end of my life. Rawson opens his eyes and says:

"Come close where I can touch you."

Not sure what to expect, I do as I am asked.

"I want to give you my thanks and blessing." He repeats the same words I had just said, and makes the Sign of the Cross on my forehead.

I am choked up. I'm afraid to open my mouth. I raise my head and see that Rawson's eyes are closed. He is sleeping. I look up to the ceiling trying to clear my blurred eyes. The world needs more people like Rawson Collins. I kiss him on the forehead. He doesn't move. I leave the room a shaken man.

Betty walks me to the door. We try to make each other feel better. She lets me out into the hall and closes the door but not before I ask her to find Rawson's sock for his bare foot.

The elevator is ten yards away. I go halfway down the hall and have to sit down. But there is no place to sit. It is quiet. I lie down on the floor and try to rest, hoping that nobody in other apartments will open a door and see me. How could I explain this?

After a few minutes I get on my knees and crawl to the elevator with the help of the wall to guide me. I push the down button and the door opens. The elevator has not been used since I arrived earlier. I don't have to wait. I couldn't stand any longer.

Patsy is in the car and comes out to help me into the front seat. I am emotionally and physically drained. The ride to our apartment takes only ten minutes. I fall asleep.

CHAPTER THIRTEEN

SERVICE FOR THE
BURIAL OF THE DEAD

Death is often associated with tragic moments in our lives. Yet Christians, from the earliest times, associate death with a time of solemn affirmation. Early saints were assured a new life by Easter and post Easter events. The prayer book service for the Burial of the Dead is, in our generation, the most loved and familiar of services in The Book of Common Prayer.

The early years of the faith were a time of testing, witnessing, and dying. Men, women and children were confronted with orders from the Roman State to adhere to the state cult which demanded obedience to the Emperor. The challenge was: Caesar or Christ! Brave souls stood tall and proclaimed, "Christ is my Lord." Many were crucified in the same manner as Jesus. Thousands were mauled, tortured, and disemboweled by lions and wild beasts in the arenas throughout the Roman Empire.

Today, I am standing under one of the many arches of the Roman Coliseum at six o'clock on a warm, humid Saturday morning. Traffic is circling at a relaxed pace as if paying homage to the thousands of Christians in the early centuries of our faith who lost their lives here. The stone walls of this ancient monument hold back the cheers of spectators and the screams of the persecuted that were heard here. For centuries, this was a place of torture and death. Within the hour the traffic will double. The pace will quicken. Horns will be blowing. European ambulances and fire trucks will bellow their cacophonous demands. Omnipresent motor bikes will veer recklessly back and forth, back and forth between our busses and speeding taxis. But for now there is a melancholic lazy presence to this spring morning.

The death of the martyrs is alive in my mind. I don't want to just dream of those days. I want to feel those long ago visions of horror, blood, pain and dignity. I want to touch courage. I want to deflect deadly claws. I want to smell fear. I want to be with them and to be one of them. These are the heroes of the faith. They were, and are today, a congregation of saints and angels who stand before me on this day in June. They turn a melancholy lazy morning into the daybreak of hope, love and faith. It is an inspired moment.

During the years of persecution no Christian was safe. *Non licet esse vos.* "It is not lawful for you to exist." Shining through this horror was the story of the resurrection. Amid the tears and moments of overwhelming fear there was a sense of victory. The intensity of this story increased the numbers of Christians throughout the Empire even though Nero and his successors tried for six generations to expunge that faith.

The church of the martyrs became a church of solemn joy. It inspired a time of hope through which we are assured by the Resurrection that loved ones are not dead but alive. The liturgy, by offering this assurance in our own time and place, helps minister to the bereaved. Certainly, Christian clergy and lay people minister together to bereaved families and friends with their own individual gifts. They visit the bereaved. They supply meals and flowers. They do chores as needed. In gentle ways friends bring love and understanding in lonely hours. But above all, a Resurrection faith in the 21st century is the same faith now as it was in the first century and it is the purpose of the funeral liturgy to speak to this important fact.

Forty seven years ago when I entered the ministry, sacramental rites were directed by prayer book rubrics, centuries old suggestions intended to guide a priest in public services. Homilies were preached by the rector or the bishop, resurrection being the central message. In my years at the seminary we were warned to be wary of those who would stray from this message of death and resurrection or worse still, allow maudlin sentiment to prevail.

Eulogies in the burial rites were frowned upon. There would have been a place in a reception area or a parish hall for friends and family, prior to the Burial Office, to give accolades and remember good times. The evening hours the night before the service when many come to pay their respects was considered a suitable time for this. These less formal meetings with family and friends offered a catharsis to help in the healing process. The force of the resurrection story would be celebrated the next day in the body of the Church.

In the seventies and eighties this tradition changed. The Burial Office in The Book of Common Prayer now empowers priests to make what they feel are meaningful substitutions in the service, but these often blur the structure and intentions of the rite and its assurances to the mourners of the "life of the world to come." There is, for example, an option in the revision of The Book of Common Prayer to replace the graceful and poetic words of the King James translation with a workbook variety of contemporary English. The opening prayer of the burial service once began, "I am the resurrection and the life, saith the Lord: he that believeth in me, though he were dead, yet shall he live; and whosoever liveth and believeth in me shall never die." Much was lost when the same prayer was reduced to, "I am the resurrection and I am life says the Lord. Whoever has faith in me shall have life even though he die. And everyone who has life and has committed himself to me in faith shall not die forever," according to the modern version. Lost were the beauty and poetry which, in themselves, offered comfort.

In the Diocese of New York, eulogies became popular. The Rt. Rev. Paul Moore, who for seventeen years was the Episcopal Bishop of New York, started giving eulogies from the pulpit of St. John the Divine. Some of his clergy assumed that if the bishop of the diocese followed this practice then it must be suitable for them to do the same. They followed the bishop's poor example. Permission was given to sons, daughters, cousins, grandchildren, nephews, nieces, and good friends to speak. Usually this practice results in disaster. It becomes "show time." Anyone with something nice to say is encouraged to enter the pulpit to say what he or she thinks. It reminds one of karaoke nights in the local town pub where anyone can come to a microphone and bellow out the words to a popular tune playing in the background.

On a warm spring Saturday morning in Cincinnati some years ago, I attended a funeral for a friend, held in a nearby suburban church. I listened to three speakers from the pulpit followed by the rector who closed the service with prayers and readings.

The first speaker was a close friend and neighbor of the deceased. He told us that, among other good things about this man, Mills was an avid sportsman who lived to hunt and fish. He had traveled around the world from the northern Arctic to African savannas to hunt big game animals. He shot numerous trophy specimens. Their heads were stuffed and now proudly displayed on the walls of his library. Mills had reported that he was kind to the animals. They did not suffer because he often killed them with one shot rather than wounding them. This was not something we needed to hear.

His son, the next speaker, said with much pride that his dad was a good Christian man even though he and his family were not church goers. As a family, they attended baptisms, weddings, and funerals.

The third speaker, a fifteen year old granddaughter, told us what a kind and generous soul her grandfather was to his family. She then paused. We waited. We watched. Tension built. An embarrassing silence ricocheted off the walls. The girl then buried her face in her hands and sobbed. I was wishing I could be somewhere else on this June day. Her father arose from the front pew and with an arm around his daughter's waist, escorted her back to the pew. It was high drama at its worst. People were wishing the service would end.

A reading from Kahlil Gibran's *The Prophet* took the place of the Old Testament lesson. A tape recorded version of The Wiffenpoof song played in the background:

> *To the tables down at Mory's*
> *To the place where Louie dwells*
> *To the dear old Temple bar we love so well*
> *Sing the Whiffenpoofs assembled with their*
> *glasses raised on high*
> *And the magic of their singing casts its spell.*

It was Mills' favorite.

The service missed the point of Christian burial. The family and the friends of Mills needed to hear about the astonishing works of God expressed in the life, death and resurrection of Jesus Christ. This ostentatious service, though well attended and endowed with endless floral arrangements, had denied the Mills family the straightforward comfort of God's tender blessing, of which they were in extreme need.

That evening I called my friend and rector of the church, who had conducted the service, to suggest a time when we might meet and talk about this service. He was embarrassed and ashamed that he had allowed the family to override what he knew to be his responsibilities to them. I commiserated with my friend on this problem that has been with many of us in the Church. Maybe a conversation with new ideas would help us both. I felt sorry for this man of God. Somewhere along the way somebody failed to explain sufficiently to our clergy that these secular practices and contemporary customs spoil our religious rites. My friend needed to know ways to avoid having this happen and to bring the bereaved to a greater understanding of the possibilities and purposes of the Office.

The funeral service for Diana, Princess of Wales took place in Westminster Abbey and had worldwide coverage. It offered a well publicized example of what can happen when the Church permits the angry or the irresponsible to give a homily. The homily, given by Diana's brother, said little of the Christian faith. What *was* said was that Diana, a loving person, was poorly treated by her in-laws. Many in the body of faith watched and listened in dismay. We questioned why the Archbishop of Canterbury did not speak and tell the good news of the resurrection. We need words of faith at these times, especially when what is happening will capture the attention of millions.

There should be a time and place to remember and recognize the famous and not-so-famous for their achievements and successes, but the burial office should not be exploited with secular demands. Let the Christian witness stand alone at the end of the eulogies and remembrances. We compromise the faith when we include secular humanism in our beliefs. One knows people who have never recovered from grief. They live the rest of their lives in a state of despair. The Reverend John Claypool has said, "There is no other experience with more lethal spiritual potential than a grief handled poorly."

Yet there is hope. Things are beginning to change. Services are once again being directed by the clergy rather than by the congregants. Parishes are beginning to set standards and rules especially in regard to weddings and funerals.

It is the Resurrection that remains the center of our faith. The first message of the new faith was sent when the apostles went to the Roman world and announced, "He is risen." This was the first message transmitted to a broken world. This is what Mills' family and friends missed on that warm spring Saturday morning in Cincinnati.

CHAPTER FOURTEEN

THE LAST DAYS

5:00 a.m. I'm staring at the ceiling in our bedroom unable to sleep. During an early shower, I notice that Father Time is continuing his countdown. I have many more yesterdays than tomorrows.

In the mirror over the sink, I see the changes in my face. Rude new thoughts interrupt my days and nights. Intruders gain momentum. The glass is fogged by steam from the shower. I use my tee shirt to wipe a circle in the center of the mirror. Within a moment, the glass closes up again. A simple act of nature becomes an omen. Could this be my life?

After coffee I return to the mirror. The glass is clear but the vision is distant. I move closer. The shadows are unnerving. Though I know his name and where he lives, the face in the mirror is a stranger. What ever happened to that excited, one-time warrior for Jesus?

"Now we see through a glass, darkly; but then face to face." (1 Corinthians 13:12).

I recalled a time in Hartford, Connecticut, looking in another mirror, in another bathroom, to see another me. There was a young man in front of a sink, reborn, full of life, joy, love, humility and honesty. That time, that afternoon, had marked a seminal change in my life history.

What has happened? I need the epiphany in Hartford of fifty years ago. Where is that sense of higher purpose that possessed and inspired me? In this dark night of my soul I would sell myself for something, someone, to speak to me about love, ambition, and hope. I need the means to fight this incredible foe—anxiety, depression, and loss. I am frightened. Am I a fair weather Christian who gives up when times are difficult?

I have spent my life encouraging others when disasters strike: death, perhaps that of a child, or of a soldier coming home in a casket, or cancer. I have counseled those overwhelmed by alcohol, infidelity, drugs and a thousand other painful situations that humans face daily and ask, "Where was God?"

I have listened to them. I have prayed with them. Often I have recommended The Book of Job in the Old Testament, one of the greatest witnesses to a life of faith that has ever been written. Job loses everything—his family his fortune, and his friends. The book is a story of human trial. It is how Job faces those trials that give meaning to life and to religion.

"For I know that my Redeemer liveth and at the last he shall stand upon this earth and my eyes shall behold him" (Job 19:25-27).

*   *   *

James Hochwalt is my doctor. I tell him that I am depressed, bored and tired. Ten years ago this same doctor saved my life. He discovered that I had a tumor and directed me to an oncologist, radiologist, and thoracic surgeon who treated me for esophageal cancer. Chemo treatments and radiology went on for weeks and then the surgeon performed his miracles on my stomach and surrounding areas. The prescribed aggressive cancer therapy cured me but wrecked the inner workings of my body. It took months before I was to get stronger. To this day my internal organs do not always understand each other. Eating remains a learning experience.

Ten years later, I find myself in my doctor's office feeling tired and worthless. I had just read a newspaper article citing research into the chemotherapy drug 5-Fluorouracil (5-FU), a commonly prescribed anti-cancer medicine used to treat cancers such as mine. For years 5-FU was, and still is, the standard of care and will probably remain that standard for years to come. It provided the basis for a cure of my cancer and that of many like me. But it can cause serious brain damage and could be responsible for side effects called "chemo brain" which include memory loss and poor concentration. It has been further demonstrated that in some patients, chemo treatments appear to trigger a serious degenerative condition in the central nervous system. The medical profession claims we are 'stuck' with what we have. The benefits of this drug outweigh the detriments for people like me but recently I have been experiencing memory loss, concentration problems, and the occasional inability to focus on a conversation. I have been wondering why, especially when I'm tired, I seem to be stuttering once again.

The doctor asks me what I am doing with my time. When I confess that my daily interests consist of reading, watching TV, listening to weather reports, and wondering what to have for dinner, he shakes his head in despair.

"Get off your butt," he orders me. "Get out of the house. Take better care of your body. Go to a gym. Walking every other day is helpful. It's important." I admitted that my only exercise is jumping to conclusions. Going to a gym with its elaborate oversized machines from outer space is not the answer for me. Walking on treadmills, laboring in rowing contraptions, swimming laps and lifting weights do not interest me. Maybe the doctors and health pundits on T.V. who proclaim that exercise will change a life are on to something. Could walking be the answer for me? It is cold in February. I do not want to walk outside. A friend suggests walking in the mall in the morning hours.

Early on a wet chilly morning, I drive to the Tri-County Mall, ten miles from home, and park in a monstrous asphalt landing zone. I head for the nearest entrance in my newly purchased Adidas sneakers. I cross the threshold into this Parthenon of stores. Even though the stores won't be open for another three hours, there are many here today because of messy weather. These people are here to walk. No one wants to be outside.

This sprawling coliseum contains over one hundred and eighty stores, most touching one another shoulder to shoulder. There are shops that dress you, others that sell you diamonds and rubies. Handbags and women's shoes for every season are favorites. On the second level there are stores with TVs, radios, electronic toys and batteries to keep the toys working. Ten dollar watches, each one different, are on display in smaller kiosks parked like gypsy wagons in the wider aisles. Sun glasses of every color, size, and shape are forever on "One Day" sales. The mall is open but the stores will remain closed until 10:00 a.m.

I am ready to feel stronger and healthier. It's show time! I begin my pilgrimage to better health hoping someone will notice my new $80 sneakers. Maybe in time I'll be the new Rocky Balboa in Cincinnati and have a statue of me erected at the entrance to the mall.

An escalator carries the overweights onto the second floor where aisles are wide and aging athletes begin the day by stepping off onto a race track. I wonder to myself if they are on steroids. They walk miles into this maze of corridors that sport kiosks, food courts, specialty stores, movie theaters, seating areas, fast food restaurants, information centers, restrooms, Macy's and Nordstrom. On and on I walk into this mélange of faces, colors, and backgrounds. Some couples speak French and others, Spanish. It is a tower of Babel. There are Asians, South Americans, Indians, Europeans, and African Americans. I pass groups of eight or ten who regularly walk together. Sometimes people pass me and say 'Good Morning.' I love this energy and variety and for a moment I forget that I am supposed to be depressed.

A large majority are fat and over sixty. Some of these AARP All Americans carry small water bottles in each hand to add weight to aging biceps. They power walk while vigorously swinging their hands up, over, sideways, up and down, ending with twisting and twirling wheelies over their heads. I am reminded of college majorettes.

"Neither snow, nor rain, nor heat nor gloom of night stay these couriers from the swift completion of their appointed rounds." Maybe these mall walkers have the answer. Do they have a vision? Are they having fun? What are they thinking about? They seem inwardly driven to succeed.

Seating areas at convenient intervals allow six to eight people to stop and rest, drink some water, or wait for a friend. For many, the mall at this hour is a big waiting room.

My cell phone rings. It will be a short call. I take the opportunity to sit in one these rest areas. An attractive older couple sits on the couch next to my chair. Both have expensive sneakers. He wears a Barbour jacket. She is classic in tartan slacks with a green neck scarf tucked into a tan wool sweater. Both have heads of snowy hair, fashionably coiffed. Slowly and carefully she helps him remove his coat, then bends over to retie the laces on his sneakers. Without looking directly at him, she continues a slow monologue in caring tones. She is romancing her husband and best friend by making a fuss over his appearance. She talks about the boys and their wives and how nice it was to have them at the home for dinner last night. His eyes stare out, still and uncomprehending. He is like a mannequin in the window behind him except that the mannequin is wearing a wide smile with eyes shining.

A young mother has stopped in the rest area and is bending over a carriage, whispering loving words and changing her baby's diaper. The baby understands nothing except that his morning nap is being interrupted by someone who loves him. Like the elderly gentleman being so tenderly cared for by his wife, the baby inhabits his own world oblivious to what is happening outside. One individual is seven months of age, the other is seventy years. Both share an isolation and innocence. Their caregivers are loving shepherds and I find myself loving both these shepherds and their sheep.

But now, something is about to change and the mall is about to be transformed. Some of the walkers are beginning to leave, perhaps to go home because they are tired, and they stop to have coffee and a donut or to read the paper before leaving.

"De Profundus," a new group arrives one by one out the depths onto the second floor, preparing for at least a two or three mile tour. Here they come!

At first, there are only a few, but within an hour these newcomers comprise an army of "yummy mummies" pushing their babies in strollers. Earlier, husbands were fed, caffeinated and sent off to work. Older children were dropped at school bus stops. The Mummies who fled their homes are now in the mall where 'wee ones' are strapped into strollers that resemble tiny tanks. The strollers are loaded with diapers, cheerios, and water bottles. Then with grim, no nonsense stares each Mummy aims for the aisle. Music heard through the earphones of an I-pod sets her pace as her day away from home begins in the freedom of the Mall.

Never giving an inch to innocent walkers, she races on. God help those in her way. Some of the strollers resemble modernized sports cars with two wheels in the rear, one in the front and a pointed prow. Our driver stares straight ahead. Walkers see what's coming and head for safety. They flatten themselves against the huge plate glass windows of the stores. This terrorist knows she is the queen of the Tri Country Mall. This is her domain. She controls the aisle. God help any one who doesn't move. This is the Cincinnati version of the Alaskan Iditarod.

Back in the area near the escalator, a mommy awaits the arrival of a friend. The two mothers meet and walk together. Now our morning arena is challenged. All eyes are set to avoid these two musher moms. Their carriages hold twins. According to a couple standing next to me, these two found each other weeks ago and have now melded into one amorphous attack chariot. "Let the games begin!" Their weapon is now a 'double wide.' The path ahead awaits them. Spectators observe their passing from the safety of the sidelines. Single carriages move aside when the feared 'double wides' approach. Today these are the queens of the sandbox, and the rules of the game inside the tri County Mall are a microcosm of the world outside.

Before I leave I want to speak to the couple in the rest stop next to the Apple computer store. I see the pair sitting on the couch holding hands, their knees touching. Their little love scene makes me want to embrace them both.

>"May I introduce myself? My name is James Leo. I am a retired priest from Cincinnati. When I was here a few minutes ago I overheard your brief conversation while you were resting. The loving manner in which you cared for each other filled me with a moment of love and affection for you both.
>
>"Here is my card. Please, please call me. I am alone in the morning hours during the week. It would be an hour of grace for me and a joy and pleasure to walk with you."
>
>"Thank you James," the woman replies. "My name is Florence. My husband is Alfred. We have been married fifty four years and would be pleased if you could be with us some morning."

I shake hands with Florence and then Alfred offers his hand and looks at me with a blank stare, saying nothing.

I leave the mall to return to my car. In two hours I have walked two miles, was a spectator at chariot races that Charlton Heston would have enjoyed, and met two people who gave a touching demonstration of what love is about. What a wonderful way to start a dreary day in Cincinnati. I say a prayer of thanksgiving for James Hochwalt who saved my life eight years earlier when he guided me through a bad bout of cancer and last week urged me to overcome my laziness and start walking. I add a prayer of thanksgiving for Florence and Alfred and for God's people in the Tri County Mall. I look forward to returning—a step perhaps, in finding hope in my life again.

Patsy

CHAPTER FIFTEEN

SMITTEN

Hidden under a Tartan skirt secured by brass and leather clasps are strong shapely legs. Probably English genes in the background. Hands and fingers are handsome and well shaped. Her body is feminine and strong. Breasts are gracious though not prominent under a blue cashmere sweater with silver buttons. The woman is possibly five foot three or four.

She is standing, left foot is forward; a brown loafer pointed faintly upward and out is slowly turning from to side to side in a small arch. The right foot behind is firmly planted, turned slightly outward. Her chin is tilted upward. Her eyes are focused on a tall man talking to her. I am sick with jealousy.

Her body is still, not moving, except for small slow sweeps of the left loafer. Hands are at rest, folded across her stomach. Dark hair, the warm color of mahogany, is trimmed stylishly short. Bangs reach down slightly over a tanned forehead.

Sex, sophistication, glamour, beauty, passion—all of these radiate from this countess, this woman of mystery.

But the face! The face is electric! The face is classic beauty. This face will surely change the lives of the host of men, women, and children that she will meet in years ahead. It may be God's grandest creation! Is she an athlete? Is she a ballerina? Would Degas seize this moment? Probably not, I conclude. Not skinny enough. Yet she floats through space. She travels within her own space. Men stare when she moves. Legs, feet, hands, arms, hair, attire—all attract, but that face is the main event. This woman walks into a room and men stand up, stop conversing, and stare. God hath wrought a Venus. Pass through fire and brimstone to see what I see and then count yourself blessed.

I follow her into the kitchen where she is bending over the oven to turn over pork chops. She asks me a question? I'm not listening. I am only looking, watching. I say "yes," hoping it's the answer to the question she has asked me. Does she know what she is doing to me? She smiles. Does this offer some vague hope of a future encounter? We move to the living room. Please God don't let me make a fool of myself.

Four months later Patricia and I are engaged, and soon after, are married. We fill our early years with laughter, passion and playing. We learn to grow up and pay attention to the needs of the Church and the family we are forming. We produce two sons who grow into outstanding men. We travel the world and experience adventures and disasters, sickness and health. Forty-seven years later we grapple with the adjustments of being alone with one another again. I still worry about making a fool of myself in her presence. I still stare at her when she walks across a room.

CHURCHES WHERE I SERVED THE SAINTS OF GOD

1962-1964—Christ Episcopal Church, Pottstown, Pennsylvania. In charge of the youth in the Parish and visiting Hill School students and faculty. Conducted my first funerals, weddings and baptisms with absolutely no finesse, piety or skill. Ended up changing diapers for Jonathan Trowbridge Leo, a new addition to our family.

1964-1966—St. John's Church, Larchmont, New York. Directed two youth groups. Started a nursery school with Peter Buchanen, an executive in a large Wall Sreet firm. Marched in Birmingham, Alabama with The Rev. Dr. Martin Luther King. Relearned the art of diaper changing when we welcomed Jason Leo into our family.

1966-1969—St. John's Episcopal Church, Cornwall, New York. First large parish where I served as the rector. The church was too small for an office so I converted the garage with a desk, chair, bench and various Bibles and prayer books. I arranged the three short shelves of books by colors separated by family photos. It made my library look larger. The church was located a few miles from West Point which enabled me to have lunch at the Officers Club. Met Major Joe Coreth, a professor in the English Department, and his wife Polly. Together the four of us encouraged other married couples at the Point to attend St. John's.

1969-1980—St. Mary's-in-Tuxedo, Tuxedo Park, New York. An aristocratic old New York congregation within the walls of a gated community an hour outside New York City. Some felt the gates in this community were to keep outsiders out. Others felt the gates were to keep the natives in. Our sons attended school in the Park. Abolished private pews and welcomed new members from the small group outside the Park who were interested in attending. A group of teenagers became active in a youth group which was fun for them and for me.

1980-1991—The American Cathedral in Paris. Served as Dean. An active congregation of people from many different countries and backgrounds who worshipped in this beautiful space: students from colleges in the United States who were participating in Junior Year Abroad Programs, members of American law firms with offices in Paris, movie and TV stars, expatriates married to Frenchmen living in Paris, U.S. Embassy employees, and numerous tourists visiting Paris. Three different Presidential visits by Reagan, Bush and Ford. Large groups of European refugees, especially from African countries. The Paris Cathedral was a mélange of people from many countries throughout the world. Rich people, poor people. People from different faiths and races. For me it was a view of the Kingdom of God. A guest register indicated people from twenty-three different countries had visited or worshipped in the Cathedral.

1991-1998—Christ Church Cathedral, Cincinnati. Dean. After designation as the Cathedral of the Diocese of Southern Ohio, extensive modernization of the entire physical plant was begun, Encouraged and guided the vestry and the Building and Grounds Committee to execute a comprehensive and costly renovation without sacrificing spiritual, fellowship, visual or artistic sensibilities. Special attention was paid to handicap and safety issues in every area of our interior and exterior structures. I offered my resignation when that work was completed. I had reached the retirement age for clergy and was healing from large doses of radiation, an extensive operation and chemo therapy for esophageal cancer. In short, I was lacking the energy which, among other assets, is absolutely necessary for this noble vocation called the priesthood. The Way of the Cross is to find that peace which passes all understanding.

A plaque on a wall near the altar reads, *"You are called a Cathedral. Now you must become a Cathedral"*.

Trinity Episcopal Church, Covington, Kentucky. A special blessing has been granted to me to be able to continue my ministry and take part in services in this active and vital parish. The leadership is strong and parishioners are enthusiastic. I love this place.

ACKNOWLEDGEMENTS

First and foremost, I thank all the wonderful people, clergy and laity alike, in all my parishes on both sides of the Atlantic. They have been my inspiration and my support.

I have been blessed as well in this endeavor by the enthusiasm of my wife Patsy and in her unerring judgment in all questions that arose.

Nonnie Denton read and made suggestions on my facts, dates, grammar, and subject matter, and in doing so, kept my spirits up and kept me going. My friend Jon Berger who works miracles and makes computer systems come alive at Procter & Gamble, gave up trying to teach me how to fish; instead he gives me a fish and sends me home after fixing my Apple Computer.

My editor Kasha Rogovy was a gold mine of tact, intelligence, humor and discretion. She always believed that I had an important story to tell, and the ability to tell it. She kept me on track and moving forward so that this day would finally arrive.